Tower
Air Fryer
Cookbook
for Beginners UK

1000 Days Crispy, Easy and Affordable Recipes for Your Whole Family and Friends with Tips & Tricks to Fry, Roast, Grill, and Bake

Reyna Towne

Warning-Disclaimer

The purpose of this book is to educate and entertain. The author or publisher does not guarantee that anyone following the techniques, suggestions, tips, ideas, or strategies will become successful. The author and publisher shall have neither liability or responsibility to anyone with respect to any loss or damage caused, or alleged to be caused, directly or indirectly by the information contained in this book.

Table of Contents

Chapter 5 Beef, Pork, and Lamb   25

Chapter 6 Fish and Seafood   32

Chapter 7 Snacks and Appetizers   40

Chapter 8 Vegetables and Sides   48

Chapter 9 Vegetarian Mains   56

Chapter 10 Desserts   60

INTRODUCTION

Hey there, I'm so excited to share my new air fryer cookbook with you all! I've always been a big fan of cooking and experimenting with new recipes, but ever since I got my hands on a Tower air fryer, it's been a total game-changer. That's why I decided to create this cookbook - to share my love for air frying and help others discover how versatile and easy it can be.

When it comes to air fryers, there are a lot of options out there. So why did I choose the Tower brand? Well, for starters, it's a UK-based company with a long-standing reputation for quality and innovation. Their air fryers are also packed with features that make cooking a breeze, like adjustable temperature controls, a large cooking capacity, and a sleek design that looks great on any countertop.

Now, you might be wondering, how exactly does an air fryer work? It's actually pretty simple - instead of using oil to cook your food, the air fryer circulates hot air around it, creating that crispy, delicious texture you love without all the added fat. It's perfect for making all kinds of dishes, from crispy chicken wings to fluffy baked potatoes and even desserts like donuts and churros.

One of the best things about using an air fryer is all the benefits it provides. Not only does it cut down on the amount of oil you use in your cooking, but it's also faster and more energy-efficient than traditional ovens. Plus, with so many different recipes to try, you'll never get bored with your meals again.

Overall, I'm so excited to share this cookbook with you and show you just how amazing air frying can be. With recipes for every occasion and every taste, you're sure to find something you love. So grab your Tower air fryer and let's get cooking!

Chapter 1 Breakfasts

Chapter 1 Breakfasts

Sausage Egg Cup

Prep time: 10 minutes | Cook time: 15 minutes | Serves 6

340 g pork sausage, removed from casings	¼ teaspoon ground black pepper
6 large eggs	½ teaspoon crushed red pepper flakes
½ teaspoon salt	

1. Place sausage in six 4-inch ramekins (about 60 g per ramekin) greased with cooking oil. Press sausage down to cover bottom and about ½-inch up the sides of ramekins. Crack one egg into each ramekin and sprinkle evenly with salt, black pepper, and red pepper flakes. 2. Place ramekins into air fryer basket. Adjust the temperature to 176°C and set the timer for 15 minutes. Egg cups will be done when sausage is fully cooked to at least 64°C and the egg is firm. Serve warm.

Breakfast Calzone

Prep time: 15 minutes | Cook time: 15 minutes | Serves 4

350 ml shredded Mozzarella cheese	4 large eggs, scrambled
120 ml blanched finely ground almond flour	230 g cooked sausage meat, removed from casings and crumbled
30 g full-fat cream cheese	8 tablespoons shredded mild
1 large whole egg	Cheddar cheese

1. In a large microwave-safe bowl, add Mozzarella, almond flour, and cream cheese. Microwave for 1 minute. Stir until the mixture is smooth and forms a ball. Add the egg and stir until dough forms. 2. Place dough between two sheets of parchment and roll out to ¼-inch thickness. Cut the dough into four rectangles. 3. Mix scrambled eggs and cooked sausage together in a large bowl. Divide the mixture evenly among each piece of dough, placing it on the lower half of the rectangle. Sprinkle each with 2 tablespoons Cheddar. 4. Fold over the rectangle to cover the egg and meat mixture. Pinch, roll, or use a wet fork to close the edges completely. 5. Cut a piece of parchment to fit your air fryer basket and place the calzones onto the parchment. Place parchment into the air fryer basket. 6. Adjust the temperature to 192°C and air fry for 15 minutes. 7. Flip the calzones halfway through the cooking time. When done, calzones should be golden in color. Serve immediately.

Savory Sweet Potato Hash

Prep time: 15 minutes | Cook time: 18 minutes | Serves 6

2 medium sweet potatoes, peeled and cut into 1-inch cubes	1 garlic clove, minced
	½ teaspoon salt
½ green pepper, diced	½ teaspoon black pepper
½ red onion, diced	½ tablespoon chopped fresh rosemary
110 g baby mushrooms, diced	
2 tablespoons olive oil	

1. Preheat the air fryer to 192°C. 2. In a large bowl, toss all ingredients together until the vegetables are well coated and seasonings distributed. 3. Pour the vegetables into the air fryer basket, making sure they are in a single even layer. (If using a smaller air fryer, you may need to do this in two batches.) 4. Roast for 9 minutes, then toss or flip the vegetables. Roast for 9 minutes more. 5. Transfer to a serving bowl or individual plates and enjoy.

Pitta and Pepperoni Pizza

Prep time: 10 minutes | Cook time: 6 minutes | Serves 1

1 teaspoon olive oil	60 ml grated Mozzarella cheese
1 tablespoon pizza sauce	¼ teaspoon garlic powder
1 pitta bread	¼ teaspoon dried oregano
6 pepperoni slices	

1. Preheat the air fryer to 176°C. Grease the air fryer basket with olive oil. 2. Spread the pizza sauce on top of the pitta bread. Put the pepperoni slices over the sauce, followed by the Mozzarella cheese. 3. Season with garlic powder and oregano. 4. Put the pitta pizza inside the air fryer and place a trivet on top. 5. Bake in the preheated air fryer for 6 minutes and serve.

Homemade Cherry Breakfast Tarts

Prep time: 15 minutes | Cook time: 20 minutes | Serves 6

Tarts:	Frosting:
2 refrigerated piecrusts	120 ml vanilla yoghurt
80 ml cherry preserves	30 g cream cheese
1 teaspoon cornflour	1 teaspoon stevia
Cooking oil	Rainbow sprinkles

Make the Tarts 1. Place the piecrusts on a flat surface. Using a knife or pizza cutter, cut each piecrust into 3 rectangles, for 6 total. (I discard the unused dough left from slicing the edges.) 2. In a small bowl, combine the preserves and cornflour. Mix well. 3. Scoop 1 tablespoon of the preserves mixture onto the top half of each piece of piecrust. 4. Fold the bottom of each piece up to close the tart. Using the back of a fork, press along the edges of each tart to seal. 5. Spray the breakfast tarts with cooking oil and place them in the air fryer. I do not recommend stacking the breakfast tarts. They will stick together if stacked. You may need to prepare them in two batches. Bake at 375ºF for 10 minutes. 6. Allow the breakfast tarts to cool fully before removing from the air fryer. 7. If necessary, repeat steps 5 and 6 for the remaining breakfast tarts. Make the Frosting 8. In a small bowl, combine the yoghurt, cream cheese, and stevia. Mix well. 9. Spread the breakfast tarts with frosting and top with sprinkles, and serve.

Chimichanga Breakfast Burrito

Prep time: 10 minutes | Cook time: 10 minutes | Serves 2

2 large (10- to 12-inch) flour tortillas	4 corn tortilla chips, crushed
120 ml canned refried beans (pinto or black work equally well)	120 ml grated chili cheese
	12 pickled jalapeño slices
	1 tablespoon vegetable oil
4 large eggs, cooked scrambled	Guacamole, salsa, and sour cream, for serving (optional)

1. Place the tortillas on a work surface and divide the refried beans between them, spreading them in a rough rectangle in the center of the tortillas. Top the beans with the scrambled eggs, crushed chips, cheese, and jalapeños. Fold one side over the fillings, then fold in each short side and roll up the rest of the way like a burrito. 2. Brush the outside of the burritos with the oil, then transfer to the air fryer, seam-side down. Air fry at 176ºC until the tortillas are browned and crisp and the filling is warm throughout, about 10 minutes. 3. Transfer the chimichangas to plates and serve warm with guacamole, salsa, and sour cream, if you like.

Mississippi Spice Muffins

Prep time: 15 minutes | Cook time: 13 minutes |
Makes 12 muffins

1 L plain flour	temperature
1 tablespoon ground cinnamon	475 ml sugar
2 teaspoons baking soda	2 large eggs, lightly beaten
2 teaspoons allspice	475 ml unsweetened applesauce
1 teaspoon ground cloves	60 ml chopped pecans
1 teaspoon salt	1 to 2 tablespoons oil
235 ml (2 sticks) butter, room	

1. In a large bowl, whisk the flour, cinnamon, baking soda, allspice, cloves, and salt until blended. 2. In another large bowl, combine the butter and sugar. Using an electric mixer, beat the mixture for 2 to 3 minutes until light and fluffy. Add the beaten eggs and stir until blended. 3. Add the flour mixture and applesauce, alternating between the two and blending after each addition. Stir in the pecans. 4. Preheat the air fryer to 164ºC. Spritz 12 silicone muffin cups with oil. 5. Pour the batter into the prepared muffin cups, filling each halfway. Place the muffins in the air fryer basket. 6. Air fry for 6 minutes. Shake the basket and air fry for 7 minutes more. The muffins are done when a toothpick inserted into the middle comes out clean.

Meritage Eggs

Prep time: 5 minutes | Cook time: 8 minutes | Serves 2

2 teaspoons unsalted butter (or coconut oil for dairy-free), for greasing the ramekins	2 tablespoons double cream (or unsweetened, unflavoured almond milk for dairy-free)
4 large eggs	3 tablespoons finely grated
2 teaspoons chopped fresh thyme	Parmesan cheese (or chive cream cheese style spread,
½ teaspoon fine sea salt	softened, for dairy-free)
¼ teaspoon ground black pepper	Fresh thyme leaves, for garnish (optional)

1. Preheat the air fryer to 204ºC. Grease two (110 g) ramekins with the butter. 2. Crack 2 eggs into each ramekin and divide the thyme, salt, and pepper between the ramekins. Pour 1 tablespoon of the heavy cream into each ramekin. Sprinkle each ramekin with 1½ tablespoons of the Parmesan cheese. 3. Place the ramekins in the air fryer and bake for 8 minutes for soft-cooked yolks (longer if you desire a harder yolk). 4. Garnish with a sprinkle of ground black pepper and thyme leaves, if desired. Best served fresh.

Turkey Sausage Breakfast Pizza

Prep time: 15 minutes | Cook time: 24 minutes | Serves 2

4 large eggs, divided	120 ml shredded low-moisture
1 tablespoon water	Mozzarella or other melting
½ teaspoon garlic powder	cheese
½ teaspoon onion granules	1 link cooked turkey sausage,
½ teaspoon dried oregano	chopped (about 60 g)
2 tablespoons coconut flour	2 sun-dried tomatoes, finely
3 tablespoons grated Parmesan	chopped
cheese	2 sping onions, thinly sliced

1. Preheat the air fryer to 204ºC. Line a cake pan with parchment paper and lightly coat the paper with olive oil. 2. In a large bowl, whisk 2 of the eggs with the water, garlic powder, onion granules, and dried oregano. Add the coconut flour, breaking up any lumps with your hands as you add it to the bowl. Stir the coconut flour into the egg mixture, mixing until smooth. Stir in the Parmesan cheese. Allow the mixture to rest for a few minutes until thick and dough-like. 3. Transfer the mixture to the prepared pan. Use a spatula to spread it evenly and slightly up the sides of the pan. Air fry until the crust is set but still light in color, about 10 minutes. Top with the cheeses, sausage, and sun-dried tomatoes. 4. Break the remaining 2 eggs into a small bowl, then slide them onto the pizza. Return the pizza to the air fryer. Air fry 10 to 14 minutes until the egg whites are set and the yolks are the desired doneness. Top with the scallions and allow to rest for 5 minutes before serving.

Breakfast Cobbler

Prep time: 20 minutes | Cook time: 30 minutes | Serves 4

Filling:	180 ml beef or chicken stock
280 g sausage meat, crumbled	Biscuits:
60 ml minced onions	3 large egg whites
2 cloves garlic, minced	180 ml blanched almond flour
½ teaspoon fine sea salt	1 teaspoon baking powder
½ teaspoon ground black	¼ teaspoon fine sea salt
pepper	2½ tablespoons very cold
1 (230 g) package cream cheese	unsalted butter, cut into ¼-inch
(or cream cheese style spread	pieces
for dairy-free), softened	Fresh thyme leaves, for garnish

1. Preheat the air fryer to 204ºC. 2. Place the sausage, onions, and garlic in a pie pan. Using your hands, break up the sausage into small pieces and spread it evenly throughout the pie pan. Season with the salt and pepper. Place the pan in the air fryer and bake for 5 minutes. 3. While the sausage cooks, place the cream cheese and stock in a food processor or blender and purée until smooth. 4. Remove the pork from the air fryer and use a fork or metal spatula to crumble it more. Pour the cream cheese mixture into the sausage and stir to combine. Set aside. 5. Make the biscuits: Place the egg whites in a medium-sized mixing bowl or the bowl of a stand mixer and whip with a hand mixer or stand mixer until stiff peaks form. 6. In a separate medium-sized bowl, whisk together the almond flour, baking powder, and salt, then cut in the butter. When you are done, the mixture should still have chunks of butter. Gently fold the flour mixture into the egg whites with a rubber spatula. 7. Use a large spoon or ice cream scoop to scoop the dough into 4 equal-sized biscuits, making sure the butter is evenly distributed. Place the biscuits on top of the sausage and cook in the air fryer for 5 minutes, then turn the heat down to 164ºC and bake for another 17 to 20 minutes, until the biscuits are golden brown. Serve garnished with fresh thyme leaves. 8. Store leftovers in an airtight container in the refrigerator for up to 3 days. Reheat in a preheated 176ºC air fryer for 5 minutes, or until warmed through.

Wholemeal Blueberry Muffins

Prep time: 10 minutes | Cook time: 15 minutes | Serves 6

Olive oil cooking spray	350 ml plus 1 tablespoon
120 ml unsweetened applesauce	wholemeal, divided
60 ml honey	½ teaspoon baking soda
120 ml non-fat plain Greek	½ teaspoon baking powder
yoghurt	½ teaspoon salt
1 teaspoon vanilla extract	120 ml blueberries, fresh or
1 large egg	frozen

1. Preheat the air fryer to 182ºC. Lightly coat the inside of six silicone muffin cups or a six-cup muffin tin with olive oil cooking spray. 2. In a large bowl, combine the applesauce, honey, yoghurt, vanilla, and egg and mix until smooth. 3. Sift in 350 ml of the flour, the baking soda, baking powder, and salt into the wet mixture, then stir until just combined. 4. In a small bowl, toss the blueberries with the remaining 1 tablespoon flour, then fold the mixture into the muffin batter. 5. Divide the mixture evenly among the prepared muffin cups and place into the basket of the air fryer. Bake for 12 to 15 minutes, or until golden brown on top and a toothpick inserted into the middle of one of the muffins comes out clean. 6. Allow to cool for 5 minutes before serving.

Bacon Eggs on the Go

Prep time: 5 minutes | Cook time: 15 minutes | Serves 1

2 eggs

110 g bacon, cooked

Salt and ground black pepper, to taste

1. Preheat the air fryer to 204°C. Put liners in a regular cupcake tin. 2. Crack an egg into each of the cups and add the bacon. Season with some pepper and salt. 3. Bake in the preheated air fryer for 15 minutes, or until the eggs are set. Serve warm.

White Bean–Oat Waffles

Prep time: 10 minutes | Cook time: 20 minutes | Serves 2

1 large egg white

2 tablespoons finely ground flaxseed

120 ml water

¼ teaspoon salt

1 teaspoon vanilla extract

120 ml cannellini beans,

drained and rinsed

1 teaspoon coconut oil

1 teaspoon liquid sweetener

120 ml old-fashioned rolled oats

Extra-virgin olive oil cooking spray

1. In a blender, combine the egg white, flaxseed, water, salt, vanilla, cannellini beans, coconut oil, and sweetener. Blend on high for 90 seconds. 2. Add the oats. Blend for 1 minute more. 3. Preheat the waffle iron. The batter will thicken to the correct consistency while the waffle iron preheats. 4. Spray the heated waffle iron with cooking spray. 5. Add 180 ml batter. Close the waffle iron. Cook for 6 to 8 minutes, or until done. Repeated with the remaining batter. 6. Serve hot, with your favorite sugar-free topping.

Lemon-Blueberry Muffins

Prep time: 5 minutes | Cook time: 20 to 25 minutes | Makes 6

muffins

300 ml almond flour

3 tablespoons granulated sweetener

1 teaspoon baking powder

2 large eggs

3 tablespoons melted butter

1 tablespoon almond milk

1 tablespoon fresh lemon juice

120 ml fresh blueberries

1. Preheat the air fryer to 176°C. Lightly coat 6 silicone muffin cups with vegetable oil. Set aside. 2. In a large mixing bowl, combine the almond flour, sweetener, and baking soda. Set aside. 3. In a separate small bowl, whisk together the eggs, butter, milk, and lemon juice. Add the egg mixture to the flour mixture and stir until just combined. Fold in the blueberries and let the batter sit for 5 minutes. 4. Spoon the muffin batter into the muffin cups, about two-thirds full. Air fry for 20 to 25 minutes, or until a toothpick inserted into the center of a muffin comes out clean. 5. Remove the basket from the air fryer and let the muffins cool for about 5 minutes before transferring them to a wire rack to cool completely.

Jalapeño Popper Egg Cups

Prep time: 10 minutes | Cook time: 10 minutes | Serves 2

4 large eggs

60 ml chopped pickled jalapeños

60 g full-fat cream cheese

120 ml shredded sharp Cheddar cheese

1. In a medium bowl, beat the eggs, then pour into four silicone muffin cups. 2. In a large microwave-safe bowl, place jalapeños, cream cheese, and Cheddar. Microwave for 30 seconds and stir. Take a spoonful, approximately ¼ of the mixture, and place it in the center of one of the egg cups. Repeat with remaining mixture. 3. Place egg cups into the air fryer basket. 4. Adjust the temperature to 160°C and bake for 10 minutes. 5. Serve warm.

Cheddar-Ham-Corn Muffins

Prep time: 10 minutes | Cook time: 6 to 8 minutes per batch | Makes 8 muffins

180 ml cornmeal/polenta

60 ml flour

1½ teaspoons baking powder

¼ teaspoon salt

1 egg, beaten

2 tablespoons rapeseed oil

120 ml milk

120 ml shredded sharp Cheddar cheese

120 ml diced ham

8 foil muffin cups, liners removed and sprayed with cooking spray

1. Preheat the air fryer to 200°C. 2. In a medium bowl, stir together the cornmeal, flour, baking powder, and salt. 3. Add egg, oil, and milk to dry ingredients and mix well. 4. Stir in shredded cheese and diced ham. 5. Divide batter among the muffin cups. 6. Place 4 filled muffin cups in air fryer basket and bake for 5 minutes. 7. Reduce temperature to 166°C and bake for 1 to 2 minutes or until toothpick inserted in center of muffin comes out clean. 8. Repeat steps 6 and 7 to cook remaining muffins.

Cheddar Soufflés

Prep time: 15 minutes | Cook time: 12 minutes | Serves 4

3 large eggs, whites and yolks separated	120 ml shredded sharp Cheddar cheese
¼ teaspoon cream of tartar	85 g cream cheese, softened

1. In a large bowl, beat egg whites together with cream of tartar until soft peaks form, about 2 minutes. 2. In a separate medium bowl, beat egg yolks, Cheddar, and cream cheese together until frothy, about 1 minute. Add egg yolk mixture to whites, gently folding until combined. 3. Pour mixture evenly into four ramekins greased with cooking spray. Place ramekins into air fryer basket. Adjust the temperature to 176°C and bake for 12 minutes. Eggs will be browned on the top and firm in the center when done. Serve warm.

Classic British Breakfast

Prep time: 5 minutes | Cook time: 25 minutes | Serves 2

235 ml potatoes, sliced and diced	1 tablespoon olive oil
475 ml baked beans	1 sausage
2 eggs	Salt, to taste

1. Preheat the air fryer to 200°C and allow to warm. 2. Break the eggs onto a baking dish and sprinkle with salt. 3. Lay the beans on the dish, next to the eggs. 4. In a bowl, coat the potatoes with the olive oil. Sprinkle with salt. 5. Transfer the bowl of potato slices to the air fryer and bake for 10 minutes. 6. Swap out the bowl of potatoes for the dish containing the eggs and beans. Bake for another 10 minutes. Cover the potatoes with parchment paper. 7. Slice up the sausage and throw the slices on top of the beans and eggs. Bake for another 5 minutes. 8. Serve with the potatoes.

Southwestern Ham Egg Cups

Prep time: 5 minutes | Cook time: 12 minutes | Serves 2

4 (30 g) slices wafer-thin ham	2 tablespoons diced red pepper
4 large eggs	2 tablespoons diced brown onion
2 tablespoons full-fat sour cream	120 ml shredded medium Cheddar cheese
60 ml diced green pepper	

1. Place one slice of ham on the bottom of four baking cups. 2. In a large bowl, whisk eggs with sour cream. Stir in green pepper, red pepper, and onion. 3. Pour the egg mixture into ham-lined baking cups. Top with Cheddar. Place cups into the air fryer basket. 4. Adjust the temperature to 160°C and bake for 12 minutes or until the tops are browned. 5. Serve warm.

All-in-One Toast

Prep time: 10 minutes | Cook time: 10 minutes | Serves 1

1 strip bacon, diced	pepper, to taste
1 slice 1-inch thick bread	60 ml grated Monterey Jack or Chedday cheese
1 egg	
Salt and freshly ground black	

1. Preheat the air fryer to 204°C. 2. Air fry the bacon for 3 minutes, shaking the basket once or twice while it cooks. Remove the bacon to a paper towel lined plate and set aside. 3. Use a sharp paring knife to score a large circle in the middle of the slice of bread, cutting halfway through, but not all the way through to the cutting board. Press down on the circle in the center of the bread slice to create an indentation. 4. Transfer the slice of bread, hole side up, to the air fryer basket. Crack the egg into the center of the bread, and season with salt and pepper. 5. Adjust the air fryer temperature to 192°C and air fry for 5 minutes. Sprinkle the grated cheese around the edges of the bread, leaving the center of the yolk uncovered, and top with the cooked bacon. Press the cheese and bacon into the bread lightly to help anchor it to the bread and prevent it from blowing around in the air fryer. 6. Air fry for one or two more minutes, just to melt the cheese and finish cooking the egg. Serve immediately.

Pancake Cake

Prep time: 10 minutes | Cook time: 7 minutes | Serves 4

120 ml blanched finely ground almond flour	softened
60 ml powdered erythritol	1 large egg
½ teaspoon baking powder	½ teaspoon unflavoured gelatin
2 tablespoons unsalted butter,	½ teaspoon vanilla extract
	½ teaspoon ground cinnamon

1. In a large bowl, mix almond flour, erythritol, and baking powder. Add butter, egg, gelatin, vanilla, and cinnamon. Pour into a round baking pan. 2. Place pan into the air fryer basket. 3. Adjust the temperature to 150°C and set the timer for 7 minutes. 4. When the cake is completely cooked, a toothpick will come out clean. Cut cake into four and serve.

Peppered Maple Bacon Knots

Prep time: 5 minutes | Cook time: 7 to 8 minutes | Serves 6

450 g maple smoked/cured bacon rashers

60 ml maple syrup

60 ml brown sugar

Coarsely cracked black peppercorns, to taste

1. Preheat the air fryer to 200℃. 2. On a clean work surface, tie each bacon strip in a loose knot. 3. Stir together the maple syrup and brown sugar in a bowl. Generously brush this mixture over the bacon knots. 4. Working in batches, arrange the bacon knots in the air fryer basket. Sprinkle with the coarsely cracked black peppercorns. 5. Air fry for 5 minutes. Flip the bacon knots and continue cooking for 2 to 3 minutes more, or until the bacon is crisp. 6. Remove from the basket to a paper towel-lined plate. Repeat with the remaining bacon knots. 7. Let the bacon knots cool for a few minutes and serve warm.

Chapter 2 Family Favorites

Chapter 2 Family Favorites

Cajun Shrimp

Prep time: 15 minutes | Cook time: 9 minutes | Serves 4

Oil, for spraying
450 g jumbo raw shrimp, peeled and deveined
1 tablespoon Cajun seasoning
170 g cooked kielbasa, cut into thick slices
½ medium courgette, cut into ¼-inch-thick slices

½ medium yellow squash or butternut squash, cut into ¼-inch-thick slices
1 green pepper, seeded and cut into 1-inch pieces
2 tablespoons olive oil
½ teaspoon salt

Preheat the air fryer to 204°C. Line the air fryer basket with parchment and spray lightly with oil. In a large bowl, toss together the shrimp and Cajun seasoning. Add the kielbasa, courgette, squash, pepper, olive oil, and salt and mix well. Transfer the mixture to the prepared basket, taking care not to overcrowd. You may need to work in batches, depending on the size of your air fryer. Cook for 9 minutes, shaking and stirring every 3 minutes. Serve immediately.

Cheesy Roasted Sweet Potatoes

Prep time: 7 minutes | Cook time: 18 to 23 minutes | Serves 4

2 large sweet potatoes, peeled and sliced
1 teaspoon olive oil
1 tablespoon white balsamic

vinegar
1 teaspoon dried thyme
60 ml grated Parmesan cheese

In a large bowl, drizzle the sweet potato slices with the olive oil and toss. Sprinkle with the balsamic vinegar and thyme and toss again. Sprinkle the potatoes with the Parmesan cheese and toss to coat. Roast the slices, in batches, in the air fryer basket at 204°C for 18 to 23 minutes, tossing the sweet potato slices in the basket once during cooking, until tender. Repeat with the remaining sweet potato slices. Serve immediately.

Steak Tips and Potatoes

Prep time: 10 minutes | Cook time: 20 minutes | Serves 4

Oil, for spraying
227 g baby gold potatoes, cut in half
½ teaspoon salt
450 g steak, cut into ½-inch pieces

1 teaspoon Worcestershire sauce
1 teaspoon granulated garlic
½ teaspoon salt
½ teaspoon freshly ground black pepper

Line the air fryer basket with parchment and spray lightly with oil. In a microwave-safe bowl, combine the potatoes and salt, then pour in about ½ inch of water. Microwave for 7 minutes, or until the potatoes are nearly tender. Drain. In a large bowl, gently mix together the steak, potatoes, Worcestershire sauce, garlic, salt, and black pepper. Spread the mixture in an even layer in the prepared basket. Air fry at 204°C for 12 to 17 minutes, stirring after 5 to 6 minutes. The cooking time will depend on the thickness of the meat and preferred doneness.

Chinese-Inspired Spareribs

Prep time: 30 minutes | Cook time: 8 minutes | Serves 4

Oil, for spraying
340 g boneless pork spareribs, cut into 3-inch-long pieces
235 ml soy sauce
180 ml sugar
120 ml beef or chicken stock

60 ml honey
2 tablespoons minced garlic
1 teaspoon ground ginger
2 drops red food colouring (optional)

Line the air fryer basket with parchment and spray lightly with oil. Combine the ribs, soy sauce, sugar, beef stock, honey, garlic, ginger, and food colouring (if using) in a large zip-top plastic bag, seal, and shake well until completely coated. Refrigerate for at least 30 minutes. Place the ribs in the prepared basket. Air fry at 192°C for 8 minutes, or until the internal temperature reaches 74°C.

Beignets

Prep time: 30 minutes | Cook time: 6 minutes | Makes 9 beignets

Oil, for greasing and spraying	235 ml milk
700 ml plain flour, plus more for dusting	2 tablespoons packed light brown sugar
1½ teaspoons salt	1 tablespoon unsalted butter
1 (2¼-teaspoon) active dry yeast	1 large egg
	235 ml icing sugar

Oil a large bowl. In a small bowl, mix together the flour, salt, and yeast. Set aside. Pour the milk into a glass measuring cup and microwave in 1-minute intervals until it boils. In a large bowl, mix together the brown sugar and butter. Pour in the hot milk and whisk until the sugar has dissolved. Let cool to room temperature. Whisk the egg into the cooled milk mixture and fold in the flour mixture until a dough forms. On a lightly floured work surface, knead the dough for 3 to 5 minutes. Place the dough in the oiled bowl and cover with a clean kitchen towel. Let rise in a warm place for about 1 hour, or until doubled in size. Roll the dough out on a lightly floured work surface until it's about ¼ inch thick. Cut the dough into 3-inch squares and place them on a lightly floured baking sheet. Cover loosely with a kitchen towel and let rise again until doubled in size, about 30 minutes. Line the air fryer basket with parchment and spray lightly with oil. Place the dough squares in the prepared basket and spray lightly with oil. You may need to work in batches, depending on the size of your air fryer. Air fry at 200ºC for 3 minutes, flip, spray with oil, and cook for another 3 minutes, until crispy. Dust with the icing sugar before serving.

Puffed Egg Tarts

Prep time: 10 minutes | Cook time: 42 minutes | Makes 4 tarts

Oil, for spraying	4 large eggs
Plain flour, for dusting	2 teaspoons chopped fresh parsley
1 (340 g) sheet frozen puff pastry, thawed	Salt and freshly ground black pepper, to taste
180 ml shredded Cheddar cheese, divided	

Preheat the air fryer to 200ºC. Line the air fryer basket with parchment and spray lightly with oil. Lightly dust your work surface with flour. Unfold the puff pastry and cut it into 4 equal squares. Place 2 squares in the prepared basket. Cook for 10 minutes. Remove the basket. Press the centre of each tart shell with a spoon to make an indentation. Sprinkle 3 tablespoons of cheese into each indentation and crack 1 egg into the centre of each tart shell. Cook for another 7 to 11 minutes, or until the eggs are cooked to your desired doneness. Repeat with the remaining puff pastry squares, cheese, and eggs. Sprinkle evenly with the parsley, and season with salt and black pepper. Serve immediately.

Steak and Vegetable Kebabs

Prep time: 15 minutes | Cook time: 5 to 7 minutes | Serves 4

2 tablespoons balsamic vinegar	340 g silverside steak, cut into 1-inch pieces
2 teaspoons olive oil	1 red pepper, sliced
½ teaspoon dried marjoram	16 button mushrooms
⅛ teaspoon freshly ground black pepper	235 ml cherry tomatoes

In a medium bowl, stir together the balsamic vinegar, olive oil, marjoram, and black pepper. Add the steak and stir to coat. Let stand for 10 minutes at room temperature. Alternating items, thread the beef, red pepper, mushrooms, and tomatoes onto 8 bamboo or metal skewers that fit in the air fryer. Air fry at 200ºC for 5 to 7 minutes, or until the beef is browned and reaches at least 64ºC on a meat thermometer. Serve immediately.

Fish and Vegetable Tacos

Prep time: 15 minutes | Cook time: 9 to 12 minutes | Serves 4

450 g white fish fillets, such as sole or cod	1 large carrot, grated
2 teaspoons olive oil	120 ml low-salt salsa
3 tablespoons freshly squeezed lemon juice, divided	80 ml low-fat Greek yoghurt
350 ml chopped red cabbage	4 soft low-salt wholemeal tortillas

Brush the fish with the olive oil and sprinkle with 1 tablespoon of lemon juice. Air fry in the air fryer basket at 200ºC for 9 to 12 minutes, or until the fish just flakes when tested with a fork. Meanwhile, in a medium bowl, stir together the remaining 2 tablespoons of lemon juice, the red cabbage, carrot, salsa, and yoghurt. When the fish is cooked, remove it from the air fryer basket and break it up into large pieces. Offer the fish, tortillas, and the cabbage mixture, and let each person assemble a taco.

Prep time: 5 minutes | Cook time: 6 minutes | Makes 36 bites

Oil, for spraying

1 (500 g) package frozen puffed pastry, thawed

235 ml granulated sugar

1 tablespoon ground cinnamon

120 ml icing sugar

1 tablespoon milk

Preheat the air fryer to 204°C. Line the air fryer basket with parchment and spray lightly with oil. Unfold the puff pastry onto a clean work surface. Using a sharp knife, cut the dough into 36 bite-size pieces. Place the dough pieces in one layer in the prepared basket, taking care not to let the pieces touch or overlap. Cook for 3 minutes, flip, and cook for another 3 minutes, or until puffed and golden. In a small bowl, mix together the granulated sugar and cinnamon. In another small bowl, whisk together the icing sugar and milk. Dredge the bites in the cinnamon-sugar mixture until evenly coated. Serve with the icing on the side for dipping.

Chapter 3 Fast and Easy Everyday Favourites

Chapter 3 Fast and Easy Everyday Favourites

Crunchy Fried Okra

Prep time: 5 minutes | Cook time: 8 to 10 minutes | Serves 4

235 ml self-raising yellow cornmeal (alternatively add 1 tablespoon baking powder to cornmeal)	1 teaspoon salt
	½ teaspoon freshly ground black pepper
1 teaspoon Italian-style seasoning	2 large eggs, beaten
1 teaspoon paprika	475 ml okra slices
	Cooking spray

Preheat the air fryer to 204ºC. Line the air fryer basket with parchment paper. In a shallow bowl, whisk the cornmeal, Italian-style seasoning, paprika, salt, and pepper until blended. Place the beaten eggs in a second shallow bowl. Add the okra to the beaten egg and stir to coat. Add the egg and okra mixture to the cornmeal mixture and stir until coated. Place the okra on the parchment and spritz it with oil. Air fry for 4 minutes. Shake the basket, spritz the okra with oil, and air fry for 4 to 6 minutes more until lightly browned and crispy. Serve immediately.

Scalloped Veggie Mix

Prep time: 10 minutes | Cook time: 15 minutes | Serves 4

1 Yukon Gold or other small white potato, thinly sliced	60 ml minced onion
	3 garlic cloves, minced
1 small sweet potato, peeled and thinly sliced	180 ml 2 percent milk
1 medium carrot, thinly sliced	2 tablespoons cornflour
	½ teaspoon dried thyme

Preheat the air fryer to 192ºC. In a baking pan, layer the potato, sweet potato, carrot, onion, and garlic. In a small bowl, whisk the milk, cornflour, and thyme until blended. Pour the milk mixture evenly over the vegetables in the pan. Bake for 15 minutes. Check the casserole—it should be golden brown on top, and the vegetables should be tender. Serve immediately.

Traditional Queso Fundido

Prep time: 10 minutes | Cook time: 25 minutes | Serves 4

110 g fresh Mexican (or Spanish if unavailable) chorizo, casings removed	475 ml shredded Oaxaca or Mozzarella cheese
1 medium onion, chopped	120 ml half-and-half (60 ml whole milk and 60 ml cream combined)
3 cloves garlic, minced	
235 ml chopped tomato	Celery sticks or tortilla chips, for serving
2 jalapeños, deseeded and diced	
2 teaspoons ground cumin	

Preheat the air fryer to 204ºC. In a baking pan, combine the chorizo, onion, garlic, tomato, jalapeños, and cumin. Stir to combine. Place the pan in the air fryer basket. Air fry for 15 minutes, or until the sausage is cooked, stirring halfway through the cooking time to break up the sausage. Add the cheese and half-and-half; stir to combine. Air fry for 10 minutes, or until the cheese has melted. Serve with celery sticks or tortilla chips.

Cheesy Baked Grits

Prep time: 10 minutes | Cook time: 12 minutes | Serves 6

180 ml hot water	½ to 1 teaspoon red pepper flakes
2 (28 g) packages instant grits	
1 large egg, beaten	235 ml shredded Cheddar cheese or jalapeño Jack cheese
1 tablespoon butter, melted	
2 cloves garlic, minced	

Preheat the air fryer to 204ºC. In a baking pan, combine the water, grits, egg, butter, garlic, and red pepper flakes. Stir until well combined. Stir in the shredded cheese. Place the pan in the air fryer basket and air fry for 12 minutes, or until the grits have cooked through and a knife inserted near the centre comes out clean. Let stand for 5 minutes before serving.

Herb-Roasted Veggies

Prep time: 10 minutes | Cook time: 14 to 18 minutes | Serves 4

1 red pepper, sliced	80 ml diced red onion
1 (230 g) package sliced mushrooms	3 garlic cloves, sliced
235 ml green beans, cut into 2-inch pieces	1 teaspoon olive oil
	½ teaspoon dried basil
	½ teaspoon dried tarragon

Preheat the air fryer to 176°C. In a medium bowl, mix the red pepper, mushrooms, green beans, red onion, and garlic. Drizzle with the olive oil. Toss to coat. Add the herbs and toss again. Place the vegetables in the air fryer basket. Roast for 14 to 18 minutes, or until tender. Serve immediately.

Air Fried Broccoli

Prep time: 5 minutes | Cook time: 6 minutes | Serves 1

4 egg yolks	Salt and pepper, to taste
60 ml butter, melted	475 ml broccoli florets
475 ml coconut flour	

Preheat the air fryer to 204°C. In a bowl, whisk the egg yolks and melted butter together. Throw in the coconut flour, salt and pepper, then stir again to combine well. Dip each broccoli floret into the mixture and place in the air fryer basket. Air fry for 6 minutes in batches if necessary. Take care when removing them from the air fryer and serve immediately.

Corn Fritters

Prep time: 15 minutes | Cook time: 8 minutes | Serves 6

235 ml self-raising flour	60 ml buttermilk
1 tablespoon sugar	180 ml corn kernels
1 teaspoon salt	60 ml minced onion
1 large egg, lightly beaten	Cooking spray

Preheat the air fryer to 176°C. Line the air fryer basket with parchment paper. In a medium bowl, whisk the flour, sugar, and salt until blended. Stir in the egg and buttermilk. Add the corn and minced onion. Mix well. Shape the corn fritter batter into 12 balls. Place the fritters on the parchment and spritz with oil. Bake for 4 minutes. Flip the fritters, spritz them with oil, and bake for 4 minutes more until firm and lightly browned. Serve immediately.

Beef Bratwursts

Prep time: 5 minutes | Cook time: 15 minutes | Serves 4

4 (85 g) beef bratwursts

Preheat the air fryer to 192°C. Place the beef bratwursts in the air fryer basket and air fry for 15 minutes, turning once halfway through. Serve hot.

Indian-Style Sweet Potato Fries

Prep time: 5 minutes | Cook time: 8 minutes | Makes 20 fries

Seasoning Mixture:	¼ teaspoon ground cayenne pepper
¾ teaspoon ground coriander	Fries:
½ teaspoon garam masala	
½ teaspoon garlic powder	2 large sweet potatoes, peeled
½ teaspoon ground cumin	2 teaspoons olive oil

Preheat the air fryer to 204°C. In a small bowl, combine the coriander, garam masala, garlic powder, cumin, and cayenne pepper. Slice the sweet potatoes into ¼-inch-thick fries. In a large bowl, toss the sliced sweet potatoes with the olive oil and the seasoning mixture. Transfer the seasoned sweet potatoes to the air fryer basket and fry for 8 minutes, until crispy. Serve warm.

Air Fried Shishito Peppers

Prep time: 5 minutes | Cook time: 5 minutes | Serves 4

230 g shishito or Padron peppers (about 24)	Coarse sea salt, to taste
	Lemon wedges, for serving
1 tablespoon olive oil	Cooking spray

Preheat the air fryer to 204°C. Spritz the air fryer basket with cooking spray. Toss the peppers with olive oil in a large bowl to coat well. Arrange the peppers in the preheated air fryer. Air fryer for 5 minutes or until blistered and lightly charred. Shake the basket and sprinkle the peppers with salt halfway through the cooking time. Transfer the peppers onto a plate and squeeze the lemon wedges on top before serving.

Air Fried Butternut Squash with Chopped Hazelnuts

Prep time: 10 minutes | Cook time: 20 minutes | Makes 700 ml

2 tablespoons whole hazelnuts

700 ml butternut squash, peeled, deseeded, and cubed

¼ teaspoon rock salt

¼ teaspoon freshly ground black pepper

2 teaspoons olive oil

Cooking spray

Preheat the air fryer to 152°C. Spritz the air fryer basket with cooking spray. Arrange the hazelnuts in the preheated air fryer. Air fry for 3 minutes or until soft. Chopped the hazelnuts roughly and transfer to a small bowl. Set aside. Set the air fryer temperature to 182°C. Spritz with cooking spray. Put the butternut squash in a large bowl, then sprinkle with salt and pepper and drizzle with olive oil. Toss to coat well. Transfer the squash in the air fryer. Air fry for 20 minutes or until the squash is soft. Shake the basket halfway through the frying time. When the frying is complete, transfer the squash onto a plate and sprinkle with chopped hazelnuts before serving.

Easy Devils on Horseback

Prep time: 5 minutes | Cook time: 7 minutes | Serves 12

24 small pitted prunes (128 g)

60 ml crumbled blue cheese, divided

8 slices centre-cut bacon, cut crosswise into thirds

Preheat the air fryer to 204°C. Halve the prunes lengthwise, but don't cut them all the way through. Place ½ teaspoon of cheese in the centre of each prune. Wrap a piece of bacon around each prune and secure the bacon with a toothpick. Working in batches, arrange a single layer of the prunes in the air fryer basket. Air fry for about 7 minutes, flipping halfway, until the bacon is cooked through and crisp. Let cool slightly and serve warm.

Sweet Corn and Carrot Fritters

Prep time: 10 minutes | Cook time: 8 to 11 minutes | Serves 4

Prep time: 10 minutes | Cook time: 8 to 11 minutes | Serves 4

Preheat the air fryer to 176°C. Place the grated carrot in a colander and press down to squeeze out any excess moisture. Dry it with a paper towel. Combine the carrots with the remaining ingredients. Mould 1 tablespoon of the mixture into a ball and press it down with your hand or a spoon to flatten it. Repeat until the rest of the mixture is used up. Spritz the balls with cooking spray. Arrange in the air fryer basket, taking care not to overlap any balls. Bake for 8 to 11 minutes, or until they're firm. Serve warm.

Chapter 4 Poultry

Chapter 4 Poultry

Sweet and Spicy Turkey Meatballs

Prep time: 15 minutes | Cook time: 15 minutes | Serves 6

Olive oil

450 g lean turkey mince

60 g whole-wheat panko bread crumbs

1 egg, beaten

1 tablespoon soy sauce

60 ml plus 1 tablespoon hoisin

sauce, divided

2 teaspoons minced garlic

⅛ teaspoon salt

⅛ teaspoon freshly ground black pepper

1 teaspoon Sriracha

1. Spray the air fryer basket lightly with olive oil. 2. In a large bowl, mix together the turkey, panko bread crumbs, egg, soy sauce, 1 tablespoon of hoisin sauce, garlic, salt, and black pepper. 3. Using a tablespoon, form 24 meatballs. 4. In a small bowl, combine the remaining 60 ml of hoisin sauce and Sriracha to make a glaze and set aside. 5. Place the meatballs in the air fryer basket in a single layer. You may need to cook them in batches. 6. Air fry at 180ºC for 8 minutes. Brush the meatballs generously with the glaze and cook until cooked through, an additional 4 to 7 minutes.

Korean Flavour Glazed Chicken Wings

Prep time: 10 minutes | Cook time: 25 minutes | Serves 4

Wings:

900 g chicken wings

1 teaspoon salt

1 teaspoon ground black pepper

Sauce:

2 tablespoons gochujang

1 tablespoon mayonnaise

1 tablespoon minced ginger

1 tablespoon minced garlic

1 teaspoon agave nectar

2 packets Splenda

1 tablespoon sesame oil

For Garnish:

2 teaspoons sesame seeds

15 g chopped green onions

1. Preheat the air fryer to 200ºC. Line a baking pan with aluminum foil, then arrange the rack on the pan. 2. On a clean work surface, rub the chicken wings with salt and ground black pepper, then arrange the seasoned wings on the rack. 3. Air fry for 20 minutes or until the wings are well browned. Flip the wings halfway through. You may need to work in batches to avoid overcrowding. 4.

Meanwhile, combine the ingredients for the sauce in a small bowl. Stir to mix well. Reserve half of the sauce in a separate bowl until ready to serve. 5. Remove the air fried chicken wings from the air fryer and toss with remaining half of the sauce to coat well. 6. Place the wings back to the air fryer and air fry for 5 more minutes or until the internal temperature of the wings reaches at least 76ºC. 7. Remove the wings from the air fryer and place on a large plate. Sprinkle with sesame seeds and green onions. Serve with reserved sauce.

Chicken, Courgette, and Spinach Salad

Prep time: 10 minutes | Cook time: 20 minutes | Serves 4

3 (140 g) boneless, skinless chicken breasts, cut into 1-inch cubes

5 teaspoons extra-virgin olive oil

½ teaspoon dried thyme

1 medium red onion, sliced

1 red bell pepper, sliced

1 small courgette, cut into strips

3 tablespoons freshly squeezed lemon juice

85 g fresh baby spinach leaves

1. Insert the crisper plate into the basket and the basket into the unit. Preheat the unit by selecting AIR ROAST, setting the temperature to 190ºC, and setting the time to 3 minutes. Select START/STOP to begin. 2. In a large bowl, combine the chicken, olive oil, and thyme. Toss to coat. Transfer to a medium metal bowl that fits into the basket. 3. Once the unit is preheated, place the bowl into the basket. 4. Select AIR ROAST, set the temperature to 190ºC, and set the time to 20 minutes. Select START/STOP to begin. 5. After 8 minutes, add the red onion, red bell pepper, and courgette to the bowl. Resume cooking. After about 6 minutes more, stir the chicken and vegetables. Resume cooking. 6. When the cooking is complete, a food thermometer inserted into the chicken should register at least 76ºC. Remove the bowl from the unit and stir in the lemon juice. 7. Put the spinach in a serving bowl and top with the chicken mixture. Toss to combine and serve immediately.

Chicken Shawarma

Prep time: 30 minutes | Cook time: 15 minutes | Serves 4

Shawarma Spice:

2 teaspoons dried oregano

1 teaspoon ground cinnamon

1 teaspoon ground cumin

1 teaspoon ground coriander

1 teaspoon kosher salt

½ teaspoon ground allspice

½ teaspoon cayenne pepper

Chicken:

450 g boneless, skinless chicken thighs, cut into large bite-size chunks

2 tablespoons vegetable oil

For Serving:

Tzatziki

Pita bread

1. For the shawarma spice: In a small bowl, combine the oregano, cayenne, cumin, coriander, salt, cinnamon, and allspice. 2. For the chicken: In a large bowl, toss together the chicken, vegetable oil, and shawarma spice to coat. Marinate at room temperature for 30 minutes or cover and refrigerate for up to 24 hours. 3. Place the chicken in the air fryer basket. Set the air fryer to 180°C for 15 minutes, or until the chicken reaches an internal temperature of 76°C. 4. Transfer the chicken to a serving platter. Serve with tzatziki and pita bread.

Brazilian Tempero Baiano Chicken Drumsticks

Prep time: 30 minutes | Cook time: 20 minutes | Serves 4

1 teaspoon cumin seeds

1 teaspoon dried oregano

1 teaspoon dried parsley

1 teaspoon ground turmeric

½ teaspoon coriander seeds

1 teaspoon kosher salt

½ teaspoon black peppercorns

½ teaspoon cayenne pepper

60 ml fresh lime juice

2 tablespoons olive oil

680 g chicken drumsticks

1. In a clean coffee grinder or spice mill, combine the cumin, oregano, parsley, turmeric, coriander seeds, salt, peppercorns, and cayenne. Process until finely ground. 2. In a small bowl, combine the ground spices with the lime juice and oil. Place the chicken in a resealable plastic bag. Add the marinade, seal, and massage until the chicken is well coated. Marinate at room temperature for 30 minutes or in the refrigerator for up to 24 hours. 3. When you are ready to cook, place the drumsticks skin side up in the air fryer basket. Set the air fryer to 200°C for 20 to 25 minutes, turning the legs halfway through the cooking time. Use a meat thermometer to ensure that the chicken has reached an internal temperature of 76°C. 4. Serve with plenty of napkins.

Coriander Chicken Kebabs

Prep time: 30 minutes | Cook time: 10 minutes | Serves 4

Chutney:

40 g unsweetened shredded coconut

120 ml hot water

40 g fresh coriander leaves, roughly chopped

10 g fresh mint leaves, roughly chopped

6 cloves garlic, roughly

chopped

1 jalapeño, seeded and roughly chopped

60-75 ml water, as needed

Juice of 1 lemon

Chicken:

450 g boneless, skinless chicken thighs, cut crosswise into thirds

Olive oil spray

1. For the chutney: In a blender or food processor, combine the coconut and hot water; set aside to soak for 5 minutes. 2. To the processor, add the coriander, mint, garlic, and jalapeño, along with 60 ml water. Blend at low speed, stopping occasionally to scrape down the sides. Add the lemon juice. With the blender or processor running, add only enough additional water to keep the contents moving. Turn the blender to high once the contents are moving freely and blend until the mixture is puréed. 3. For the chicken: Place the chicken pieces in a large bowl. Add ¼ cup of the chutney and mix well to coat. Set aside the remaining chutney to use as a dip. Marinate the chicken for 15 minutes at room temperature. 4. Spray the air fryer basket with olive oil spray. Arrange the chicken in the air fryer basket. Set the air fryer to 180°C for 10 minutes. Use a meat thermometer to ensure that the chicken has reached an internal temperature of 76°C. 5. Serve the chicken with the remaining chutney.

Chipotle Aioli Wings

Prep time: 5 minutes | Cook time: 25 minutes | Serves 6

900 g bone-in chicken wings

½ teaspoon salt

¼ teaspoon ground black pepper

2 tablespoons mayonnaise

2 teaspoons chipotle powder

2 tablespoons lemon juice

1. In a large bowl, toss wings in salt and pepper, then place into ungreased air fryer basket. Adjust the temperature to 200°C and air fry for 25 minutes, shaking the basket twice while cooking. Wings will be done when golden and have an internal temperature of at least 76°C. 2. In a small bowl, whisk together mayonnaise, chipotle powder, and lemon juice. Place cooked wings into a large serving bowl and drizzle with aioli. Toss to coat. Serve warm.

Italian Flavour Chicken Breasts with Roma Tomatoes

Prep time: 10 minutes | Cook time: 60 minutes | Serves 8

1.4 kg chicken breasts, bone-in	½ teaspoon salt
1 teaspoon minced fresh basil	½ teaspoon freshly ground
1 teaspoon minced fresh rosemary	black pepper
2 tablespoons minced fresh parsley	4 medium Roma tomatoes, halved
1 teaspoon cayenne pepper	Cooking spray

1. Preheat the air fryer to 190ºC. Spritz the air fryer basket with cooking spray. 2. Combine all the ingredients, except for the chicken breasts and tomatoes, in a large bowl. Stir to mix well. 3. Dunk the chicken breasts in the mixture and press to coat well. 4. Transfer the chicken breasts in the preheated air fryer. You may need to work in batches to avoid overcrowding. 5. Air fry for 25 minutes or until the internal temperature of the thickest part of the breasts reaches at least 76ºC. Flip the breasts halfway through the cooking time. 6. Remove the cooked chicken breasts from the basket and adjust the temperature to 180ºC. 7. Place the tomatoes in the air fryer and spritz with cooking spray. Sprinkle with a touch of salt and cook for 10 minutes or until tender. Shake the basket halfway through the cooking time. 8. Serve the tomatoes with chicken breasts on a large serving plate.

Butter and Bacon Chicken

Prep time: 10 minutes | Cook time: 65 minutes | Serves 6

1 (1.8 kg) whole chicken	1 teaspoon salt
2 tablespoons salted butter, softened	½ teaspoon ground black pepper
1 teaspoon dried thyme	6 slices sugar-free bacon
½ teaspoon garlic powder	

1. Pat chicken dry with a paper towel, then rub with butter on all sides. Sprinkle thyme, garlic powder, salt, and pepper over chicken. 2. Place chicken into ungreased air fryer basket, breast side up. Lay strips of bacon over chicken and secure with toothpicks. 3. Adjust the temperature to 180ºC and air fry for 65 minutes. Halfway through cooking, remove and set aside bacon and flip chicken over. Chicken will be done when the skin is golden and crispy and the internal temperature is at least 76ºC. Serve warm with bacon.

One-Dish Chicken and Rice

Prep time: 10 minutes | Cook time: 40 minutes | Serves 4

190 g long-grain white rice, rinsed and drained	3 cloves garlic, minced
120 g cut frozen green beans (do not thaw)	1 tablespoon toasted sesame oil
1 tablespoon minced fresh ginger	1 teaspoon kosher salt
	1 teaspoon black pepper
	450 g chicken wings, preferably drumettes

1. In a baking pan, combine the rice, green beans, ginger, garlic, sesame oil, salt, and pepper. Stir to combine. Place the chicken wings on top of the rice mixture. 2. Cover the pan with foil. Make a long slash in the foil to allow the pan to vent steam. Place the pan in the air fryer basket. Set the air fryer to (190ºC for 30 minutes. 3. Remove the foil. Set the air fryer to 200ºC for 10 minutes, or until the wings have browned and rendered fat into the rice and vegetables, turning the wings halfway through the cooking time.

Herbed Turkey Breast with Simple Dijon Sauce

Prep time: 5 minutes | Cook time: 30 minutes | Serves 4

1 teaspoon chopped fresh sage	1½ teaspoons sea salt
1 teaspoon chopped fresh tarragon	1 teaspoon ground black pepper
1 teaspoon chopped fresh thyme leaves	1 (900 g) turkey breast
1 teaspoon chopped fresh rosemary leaves	3 tablespoons Dijon mustard
	3 tablespoons butter, melted
	Cooking spray

1. Preheat the air fryer to 200ºC. Spritz the air fryer basket with cooking spray. 2. Combine the herbs, salt, and black pepper in a small bowl. Stir to mix well. Set aside. 3. Combine the Dijon mustard and butter in a separate bowl. Stir to mix well. 4. Rub the turkey with the herb mixture on a clean work surface, then brush the turkey with Dijon mixture. 5. Arrange the turkey in the preheated air fryer basket. Air fry for 30 minutes or until an instant-read thermometer inserted in the thickest part of the turkey breast reaches at least 76ºC. 6. Transfer the cooked turkey breast on a large plate and slice to serve.

Blackened Cajun Chicken Tenders

Prep time: 10 minutes | Cook time: 17 minutes | Serves 4

2 teaspoons paprika	pepper
1 teaspoon chili powder	2 tablespoons coconut oil
½ teaspoon garlic powder	450 g boneless, skinless chicken
½ teaspoon dried thyme	tenders
¼ teaspoon onion powder	60 ml full-fat ranch dressing
⅛ teaspoon ground cayenne	

1. In a small bowl, combine all seasonings. 2. Drizzle oil over chicken tenders and then generously coat each tender in the spice mixture. Place tenders into the air fryer basket. 3. Adjust the temperature to (190°C and air fry for 17 minutes. 4. Tenders will be 76°C internally when fully cooked. Serve with ranch dressing for dipping.

Thai Tacos with Peanut Sauce

Prep time: 10 minutes | Cook time: 6 minutes | Serves 4

450 g chicken mince	2 tablespoons wheat-free tamari
10 g diced onions (about 1	or coconut aminos
small onion)	1½ teaspoons hot sauce
2 cloves garlic, minced	5 drops liquid stevia (optional)
¼ teaspoon fine sea salt	For Serving:
Sauce:	2 small heads butter lettuce,
60 g creamy peanut butter,	leaves separated
room temperature	Lime slices (optional)
2 tablespoons chicken broth,	For Garnish (Optional):
plus more if needed	Coriander leaves
2 tablespoons lime juice	Shredded purple cabbage
2 tablespoons grated fresh	Sliced green onions
ginger	

1. Preheat the air fryer to 180°C. . 2. Place the chicken mince, onions, garlic, and salt in a pie pan or a dish that will fit in your air fryer. Break up the chicken with a spatula. Place in the air fryer and bake for 5 minutes, or until the chicken is browned and cooked through. Break up the chicken again into small crumbles. 3. Make the sauce. In a medium-sized bowl, stir together the peanut butter, broth, lime juice, ginger, tamari, hot sauce, and stevia (if using) until well combined. If the sauce is too thick, add another tablespoon or two of broth. Taste and add more hot sauce if desired. 4. Add half of the sauce to the pan with the chicken. Cook for another minute, until heated through, and stir well to combine. 5. Assemble the tacos: Place several lettuce leaves on a serving plate.

Place a few tablespoons of the chicken mixture in each lettuce leaf and garnish with coriander leaves, purple cabbage, and sliced green onions, if desired. Serve the remaining sauce on the side. Serve with lime slices, if desired. 6. Store leftover meat mixture in an airtight container in the refrigerator for up to 4 days; store leftover sauce, lettuce leaves, and garnishes separately. Reheat the meat mixture in a lightly greased pie pan in a preheated 180°C air fryer for 3 minutes, or until heated through.

Chicken Pesto Parmigiana

Prep time: 10 minutes | Cook time: 23 minutes | Serves 4

2 large eggs	pounded to ¼ inch thick
1 tablespoon water	65 g pesto
Fine sea salt and ground black	115 g shredded Mozzarella
pepper, to taste	cheese
85 g powdered Parmesan	Finely chopped fresh basil, for
cheese	garnish (optional)
2 teaspoons Italian seasoning	Grape tomatoes, halved, for
4 (140 g) boneless, skinless	serving (optional)
chicken breasts or thighs,	

1. Spray the air fryer basket with avocado oil. Preheat the air fryer to 200°C. 2. Crack the eggs into a shallow baking dish, add the water and a pinch each of salt and pepper, and whisk to combine. In another shallow baking dish, stir together the Parmesan and Italian seasoning until well combined. 3. Season the chicken breasts well on both sides with salt and pepper. Dip one chicken breast in the eggs and let any excess drip off, then dredge both sides of the breast in the Parmesan mixture. Spray the breast with avocado oil and place it in the air fryer basket. Repeat with the remaining 3 chicken breasts. 4. Air fry the chicken in the air fryer for 20 minutes, or until the internal temperature reaches 76°C and the breading is golden brown, flipping halfway through. 5. Dollop each chicken breast with ¼ of the pesto and top with the Mozzarella. Return the breasts to the air fryer and cook for 3 minutes, or until the cheese is melted. Garnish with basil and serve with halved grape tomatoes on the side, if desired. 6. Store leftovers in an airtight container in the refrigerator for up to 4 days. Reheat in a preheated 200°C air fryer for 5 minutes, or until warmed through.

Chicken Paillard

Prep time: 10 minutes | Cook time: 10 minutes | Serves 2

2 large eggs, room temperature	Lemon Butter Sauce:
1 tablespoon water	2 tablespoons unsalted butter,
40 g powdered Parmesan	melted
cheese or pork dust	2 teaspoons lemon juice
2 teaspoons dried thyme leaves	¼ teaspoon finely chopped
1 teaspoon ground black pepper	fresh thyme leaves, plus more
2 (140 g) boneless, skinless	for garnish
chicken breasts, pounded to ½	⅛ teaspoon fine sea salt
inch thick	Lemon slices, for serving

1. Spray the air fryer basket with avocado oil. Preheat the air fryer to 200ºC. 2. Beat the eggs in a shallow dish, then add the water and stir well. 3. In a separate shallow dish, mix together the Parmesan, thyme, and pepper until well combined. 4. One at a time, dip the chicken breasts in the eggs and let any excess drip off, then dredge both sides of the chicken in the Parmesan mixture. As you finish, set the coated chicken in the air fryer basket. 5. Roast the chicken in the air fryer for 5 minutes, then flip the chicken and cook for another 5 minutes, or until cooked through and the internal temperature reaches 76ºC. 6. While the chicken cooks, make the lemon butter sauce: In a small bowl, mix together all the sauce ingredients until well combined. 7. Plate the chicken and pour the sauce over it. Garnish with chopped fresh thyme and serve with lemon slices. 8. Store leftovers in an airtight container in the refrigerator for up to 4 days. Reheat in a preheated 200ºC air fryer for 5 minutes, or until heated through.

Spinach and Feta Stuffed Chicken Breasts

Prep time: 10 minutes | Cook time: 27 minutes | Serves 4

1 (280 g) package frozen	black pepper
spinach, thawed and drained	4 boneless chicken breasts
well	Salt and freshly ground black
80 g feta cheese, crumbled	pepper, to taste
½ teaspoon freshly ground	1 tablespoon olive oil

1. Prepare the filling. Squeeze out as much liquid as possible from the thawed spinach. Rough chop the spinach and transfer it to a mixing bowl with the feta cheese and the freshly ground black pepper. 2. Prepare the chicken breast. Place the chicken breast on a cutting board and press down on the chicken breast with one hand to keep it stabilized. Make an incision about 1-inch long in the fattest side of the breast. Move the knife up and down inside the

chicken breast, without poking through either the top or the bottom, or the other side of the breast. The inside pocket should be about 3-inches long, but the opening should only be about 1-inch wide. If this is too difficult, you can make the incision longer, but you will have to be more careful when cooking the chicken breast since this will expose more of the stuffing. 3. Once you have prepared the chicken breasts, use your fingers to stuff the filling into each pocket, spreading the mixture down as far as you can. 4. Preheat the air fryer to 190ºC. 5. Lightly brush or spray the air fryer basket and the chicken breasts with olive oil. Transfer two of the stuffed chicken breasts to the air fryer. Air fry for 12 minutes, turning the chicken breasts over halfway through the cooking time. Remove the chicken to a resting plate and air fry the second two breasts for 12 minutes. Return the first batch of chicken to the air fryer with the second batch and air fry for 3 more minutes. When the chicken is cooked, an instant read thermometer should register 76ºC in the thickest part of the chicken, as well as in the stuffing. 6. Remove the chicken breasts and let them rest on a cutting board for 2 to 3 minutes. Slice the chicken on the bias and serve with the slices fanned out.

Apricot-Glazed Chicken Drumsticks

Prep time: 15 minutes | Cook time: 30 minutes | Makes 6 drumsticks

For the Glaze:	6 chicken drumsticks
160 g apricot preserves	½ teaspoon seasoning salt
½ teaspoon tamari	1 teaspoon salt
¼ teaspoon chili powder	½ teaspoon ground black
2 teaspoons Dijon mustard	pepper
For the Chicken:	Cooking spray

Make the glaze: 1. Combine the ingredients for the glaze in a saucepan, then heat over low heat for 10 minutes or until thickened. 2. Turn off the heat and sit until ready to use. Make the Chicken: 1. Preheat the air fryer to 190ºC. Spritz the air fryer basket with cooking spray. 2. Combine the seasoning salt, salt, and pepper in a small bowl. Stir to mix well. 3. Place the chicken drumsticks in the preheated air fryer. Spritz with cooking spray and sprinkle with the salt mixture on both sides. 4. Air fry for 20 minutes or until well browned. Flip the chicken halfway through. 5. Baste the chicken with the glaze and air fryer for 2 more minutes or until the chicken tenderloin is glossy. 6. Serve immediately.

Nacho Chicken Fries

Prep time: 20 minutes | Cook time: 6 to 7 minutes per batch | Serves 4 to 6

450 g chicken tenders	Oil for misting or cooking spray
Salt, to taste	Seasoning Mix:
30 g flour	1 tablespoon chili powder
2 eggs	1 teaspoon ground cumin
90 g panko bread crumbs	½ teaspoon garlic powder
20 g crushed organic nacho cheese tortilla chips	½ teaspoon onion powder

1. Stir together all seasonings in a small cup and set aside. 2. Cut chicken tenders in half crosswise, then cut into strips no wider than about ½ inch. 3. Preheat the air fryer to 200ºC. 4. Salt chicken to taste. Place strips in large bowl and sprinkle with 1 tablespoon of the seasoning mix. Stir well to distribute seasonings. 5. Add flour to chicken and stir well to coat all sides. 6. Beat eggs together in a shallow dish. 7. In a second shallow dish, combine the panko, crushed chips, and the remaining 2 teaspoons of seasoning mix. 8. Dip chicken strips in eggs, then roll in crumbs. Mist with oil or cooking spray. 9. Chicken strips will cook best if done in two batches. They can be crowded and overlapping a little but not stacked in double or triple layers. 10. Cook for 4 minutes. Shake basket, mist with oil, and cook 2 to 3 more minutes, until chicken juices run clear and outside is crispy. 11. Repeat step 10 to cook remaining chicken fries.

Chicken and Broccoli Casserole

Prep time: 5 minutes | Cook time: 20 to 25 minutes | Serves 4

230 g broccoli, chopped into florets	½ teaspoon garlic powder
280 g shredded cooked chicken	Salt and freshly ground black pepper, to taste
115 g cream cheese	2 tablespoons chopped fresh basil
80 g heavy cream	
1½ teaspoons Dijon mustard	230 g shredded Cheddar cheese

1. Preheat the air fryer to 200ºC. Lightly coat a casserole dish that will fit in air fryer, with olive oil and set aside. 2. Place the broccoli in a large glass bowl with 1 tablespoon of water and cover with a microwavable plate. Microwave on high for 2 to 3 minutes until the broccoli is bright green but not mushy. Drain if necessary and add to another large bowl along with the shredded chicken. 3. In the same glass bowl used to microwave the broccoli, combine the cream cheese and cream. Microwave for 30 seconds to 1 minute on high and stir until smooth. Add the mustard and garlic powder and season to taste with salt and freshly ground black pepper. Whisk until the sauce is smooth. 4. Pour the warm sauce over the broccoli and chicken mixture and then add the basil. Using a silicone spatula, gently fold the mixture until thoroughly combined. 5. Transfer the chicken mixture to the prepared casserole dish and top with the cheese. Air fry for 20 to 25 minutes until warmed through and the cheese has browned.

Buffalo Crispy Chicken Strips

Prep time: 15 minutes | Cook time: 13 to 17 minutes per batch | Serves 4

90 g all-purpose flour	pepper
2 eggs	16 chicken breast strips, or 3 large boneless, skinless chicken breasts, cut into 1-inch strips
2 tablespoons water	
120 g seasoned panko bread crumbs	
2 teaspoons granulated garlic	Olive oil spray
1 teaspoon salt	60 ml Buffalo sauce, plus more as needed
1 teaspoon freshly ground black	

1. Put the flour in a small bowl. 2. In another small bowl, whisk the eggs and the water. 3. In a third bowl, stir together the panko, granulated garlic, salt, and pepper. 4. Dip each chicken strip in the flour, in the egg, and in the panko mixture to coat. Press the crumbs onto the chicken with your fingers. 5. Insert the crisper plate into the basket and the basket into the unit. Preheat the unit by selecting AIR FRY, setting the temperature to 190ºC, and setting the time to 3 minutes. Select START/STOP to begin. 6. Once the unit is preheated, place a parchment paper liner into the basket. Working in batches if needed, place the chicken strips into the basket. Do not stack unless using a wire rack for the second layer. Spray the top of the chicken with olive oil. 7. Select AIR FRY, set the temperature to 190ºC, and set the time to 17 minutes. Select START/STOP to begin. 8. After 10 or 12 minutes, remove the basket, flip the chicken, and spray again with olive oil. Reinsert the basket to resume cooking. 9. When the cooking is complete, the chicken should be golden brown and crispy and a food thermometer inserted into the chicken should register 76ºC. 10. Repeat steps 6, 7, and 8 with any remaining chicken. 11. Transfer the chicken to a large bowl. Drizzle the Buffalo sauce over the top of the cooked chicken, toss to coat, and serve.

Spanish Chicken and Mini Sweet Pepper Baguette

Prep time: 10 minutes | Cook time: 20 minutes | Serves 2

570 g assorted small chicken parts, breasts cut into halves

¼ teaspoon salt

¼ teaspoon ground black pepper

2 teaspoons olive oil

230 g mini sweet peppers

60 g light mayonnaise

¼ teaspoon smoked paprika

½ clove garlic, crushed

Baguette, for serving

Cooking spray

1. Preheat air fryer to 190ºC. Spritz the air fryer basket with cooking spray. 2. Toss the chicken with salt, ground black pepper, and olive oil in a large bowl. 3. Arrange the sweet peppers and chicken in the preheated air fryer and air fry for 10 minutes, then transfer the peppers on a plate. 4. Flip the chicken and air fry for 10 more minutes or until well browned. 5. Meanwhile, combine the mayo, paprika, and garlic in a small bowl. Stir to mix well. 6. Assemble the baguette with chicken and sweet pepper, then spread with mayo mixture and serve.

Yellow Curry Chicken Thighs with Peanuts

Prep time: 10 minutes | Cook time: 20 minutes | Serves 6

120 ml unsweetened full-fat coconut milk

2 tablespoons yellow curry paste

1 tablespoon minced fresh ginger

1 tablespoon minced garlic

1 teaspoon kosher salt

450 g boneless, skinless chicken thighs, halved crosswise

2 tablespoons chopped peanuts

1. In a large bowl, stir together the coconut milk, curry paste, ginger, garlic, and salt until well blended. Add the chicken; toss well to coat. Marinate at room temperature for 30 minutes, or cover and refrigerate for up to 24 hours. 2. Preheat the air fryer to 190ºC. 3. Place the chicken (along with marinade) in a baking pan. Place the pan in the air fryer basket. Bake for 20 minutes, turning the chicken halfway through the cooking time. Use a meat thermometer to ensure the chicken has reached an internal temperature of 76ºC. 4. Sprinkle the chicken with the chopped peanuts and serve.

Chapter 5 Beef, Pork, and Lamb

Chapter 5 Beef, Pork, and Lamb

Cheddar Bacon Burst with Spinach

Prep time: 5 minutes | Cook time: 60 minutes | Serves 8

30 slices bacon	2 teaspoons Italian seasoning
1 tablespoon Chipotle chilli powder	120 ml Cheddar cheese
	1 L raw spinach

1. Preheat the air fryer to 192°C. 2. Weave the bacon into 15 vertical pieces and 12 horizontal pieces. Cut the extra 3 in half to fill in the rest, horizontally. 3. Season the bacon with Chipotle chilli powder and Italian seasoning. 4. Add the cheese to the bacon. 5. Add the spinach and press down to compress. 6. Tightly roll up the woven bacon. 7. Line a baking sheet with kitchen foil and add plenty of salt to it. 8. Put the bacon on top of a cooling rack and put that on top of the baking sheet. 9. Bake for 60 minutes. 10. Let cool for 15 minutes before slicing and serving.

Short Ribs with Chimichurri

Prep time: 30 minutes | Cook time: 13 minutes | Serves 4

450 g boneless short ribs	1 tablespoon freshly squeezed lemon juice
1½ teaspoons sea salt, divided	
½ teaspoon freshly ground black pepper, divided	½ teaspoon ground cumin
120 ml fresh parsley leaves	¼ teaspoon red pepper flakes
120 ml fresh coriander leaves	2 tablespoons extra-virgin olive oil
1 teaspoon minced garlic	Avocado oil spray

1. Pat the short ribs dry with paper towels. Sprinkle the ribs all over with 1 teaspoon salt and ¼ teaspoon black pepper. Let sit at room temperature for 45 minutes. 2. Meanwhile, place the parsley, coriander, garlic, lemon juice, cumin, red pepper flakes, the remaining ½ teaspoon salt, and the remaining ¼ teaspoon black pepper in a blender or food processor. With the blender running, slowly drizzle in the olive oil. Blend for about 1 minute, until the mixture is smooth and well combined. 3. Set the air fryer to 204°C. Spray both sides of the ribs with oil. Place in the basket and air fry for 8 minutes. Flip and cook for another 5 minutes, until an instant-read thermometer reads 52°C for medium-rare (or to your desired

doneness). 4. Allow the meat to rest for 5 to 10 minutes, then slice. Serve warm with the chimichurri sauce.

Tuscan Air Fried Veal Loin

Prep time: 1 hour 10 minutes | Cook time: 12 minutes | Makes 3 veal chops

1½ teaspoons crushed fennel seeds	1½ teaspoons salt
	½ teaspoon red pepper flakes
1 tablespoon minced fresh rosemary leaves	2 tablespoons olive oil
1 tablespoon minced garlic	3 (280 g) bone-in veal loin, about ½ inch thick
1½ teaspoons lemon zest	

1. Combine all the ingredients, except for the veal loin, in a large bowl. Stir to mix well. 2. Dunk the loin in the mixture and press to submerge. Wrap the bowl in plastic and refrigerate for at least an hour to marinate. 3. Preheat the air fryer to 204°C. 4. Arrange the veal loin in the preheated air fryer and air fry for 12 minutes for medium-rare, or until it reaches your desired doneness. 5. Serve immediately.

Easy Lamb Chops with Asparagus

Prep time: 10 minutes | Cook time: 15 minutes | Serves 4

4 asparagus spears, trimmed	2 teaspoons chopped fresh thyme, for serving
2 tablespoons olive oil, divided	
450 g lamb chops	Salt and ground black pepper, to taste
1 garlic clove, minced	

1. Preheat the air fryer to 204°C. Spritz the air fryer basket with cooking spray. 2. On a large plate, brush the asparagus with 1 tablespoon olive oil, then sprinkle with salt. Set aside. 3. On a separate plate, brush the lamb chops with remaining olive oil and sprinkle with salt and ground black pepper. 4. Arrange the lamb chops in the preheated air fryer. Air fry for 10 minutes. 5. Flip the lamb chops and add the asparagus and garlic. Air fry for 5 more minutes or until the lamb is well browned and the asparagus is tender. 6. Serve them on a plate with thyme on top.

Chicken Fried Steak with Cream Gravy

Prep time: 5 minutes | Cook time: 10 minutes | Serves 4

4 small thin minute steaks	Cream Gravy:
(about 450 g)	120 mldouble cream
½ teaspoon salt	60 g cream cheese
½ teaspoon freshly ground	60 ml bacon fat
black pepper	2 to 3 tablespoons water
¼ teaspoon garlic powder	2 to 3 dashes Worcestershire
1 egg, lightly beaten	sauce
235 ml crushed pork scratchings	Salt and freshly ground black
(about 85 g)	pepper, to taste

1. Preheat the air fryer to 204ºC. 2. Working one at a time, place the steak between two sheets of parchment paper and use a meat mallet to pound to an even thickness. 3. In a small bowl, combine the salt, pepper, and garlic power. Season both sides of each steak with the mixture. 4. Place the egg in a small shallow dish and the pork rinds in another small shallow dish. Dip each steak first in the egg wash, followed by the pork scratchings, pressing lightly to form an even coating. Working in batches if necessary, arrange the steaks in a single layer in the air fryer basket. Air fry for 10 minutes until crispy and cooked through. 5. To make the cream gravy: In a heavy-bottomed pot, warm the cream, cream cheese, and bacon fat over medium heat, whisking until smooth. Lower the heat if the mixture begins to boil. Continue whisking as you slowly add the water, 1 tablespoon at a time, until the sauce reaches the desired consistency. Season with the Worcestershire sauce and salt and pepper to taste. Serve over the chicken fried steaks.

Mongolian-Style Beef

Prep time: 10 minutes | Cook time: 10 minutes | Serves 4

Oil, for spraying	2 teaspoons toasted sesame oil
60 ml cornflour	1 tablespoon minced garlic
450 g bavette or skirt steak,	½ teaspoon ground ginger
thinly sliced	120 ml water
180 ml packed light brown	Cooked white rice or ramen
sugar	noodles, for serving
120 ml soy sauce	

1. Line the air fryer basket with parchment and spray lightly with oil. 2. Place the cornflour in a bowl and dredge the steak until evenly coated. Shake off any excess cornflour. 3. Place the steak in the prepared basket and spray lightly with oil. 4. Roast at 200ºC for 5 minutes, flip, and cook for another 5 minutes. 5. In a small saucepan, combine the brown sugar, soy sauce, sesame oil, garlic, ginger, and water and bring to a boil over medium-high heat, stirring frequently. Remove from the heat. 6. Transfer the meat to the sauce and toss until evenly coated. Let sit for about 5 minutes so the steak absorbs the flavors. Serve with white rice or ramen noodles.

Fruited Ham

Prep time: 15 minutes | Cook time: 8 to 10 minutes | Serves 4

235 ml orange marmalade	450 g cooked ham, cut into
60 ml packed light brown sugar	1-inch cubes
¼ teaspoon ground cloves	120 ml canned mandarin
½ teaspoon mustard powder	oranges, drained and chopped
1 to 2 tablespoons oil	

1. In a small bowl, stir together the orange marmalade, brown sugar, cloves, and mustard powder until blended. Set aside. 2. Preheat the air fryer to 160ºC. Spritz a baking pan with oil. 3. Place the ham cubes in the prepared pan. Pour the marmalade sauce over the ham to glaze it. 4. Cook for 4 minutes. Stir and cook for 2 minutes more. 5. Add the mandarin oranges and cook for 2 to 4 minutes more until the sauce begins to thicken and the ham is tender.

Rosemary Roast Beef

Prep time: 30 minutes | Cook time: 30 to 35 minutes | Serves 8

1 (900 g) beef roasting joint,	2 teaspoons minced garlic
tied with kitchen string	2 tablespoons finely chopped
Sea salt and freshly ground	fresh rosemary
black pepper, to taste	60 ml avocado oil

1. Season the roast generously with salt and pepper. 2. In a small bowl, whisk together the garlic, rosemary, and avocado oil. Rub this all over the roast. Cover loosely with aluminum foil or plastic wrap and refrigerate for at least 12 hours or up to 2 days. 3. Remove the roast from the refrigerator and allow to sit at room temperature for about 1 hour. 4. Set the air fryer to 164ºC. Place the roast in the air fryer basket and roast for 15 minutes. Flip the roast and cook for 15 to 20 minutes more, until the meat is browned and an instant-read thermometer reads 49ºC at the thickest part (for medium-rare). 5. Transfer the meat to a cutting board, and let it rest for 15 minutes before thinly slicing and serving.

Filipino Crispy Pork Belly

Prep time: 20 minutes | Cook time: 30 minutes | Serves 4

450 g pork belly	1 teaspoon coarse or flaky salt
700 ml water	1 teaspoon black pepper
6 garlic cloves	2 bay leaves
2 tablespoons soy sauce	

1. Cut the pork belly into three thick chunks so it will cook more evenly. 2. Place the pork, water, garlic, soy sauce, salt, pepper, and bay leaves in the inner pot of an Instant Pot or other electric pressure cooker. Seal and cook at high pressure for 15 minutes. Let the pressure release naturally for 10 minutes, then manually release the remaining pressure. (If you do not have a pressure cooker, place all the ingredients in a large saucepan. Cover and cook over low heat until a knife can be easily inserted into the skin side of pork belly, about 1 hour.) Using tongs, very carefully transfer the meat to a wire rack over a rimmed baking sheet to drain and dry for 10 minutes. 3. Cut each chunk of pork belly into two long slices. Arrange the slices in the air fryer basket. Set the air fryer to 204°C for 15 minutes, or until the fat has crisped. 4. Serve immediately.

Italian Sausages with Peppers and Onions

Prep time: 5 minutes | Cook time: 28 minutes | Serves 3

1 medium onion, thinly sliced	coconut oil
1 yellow or orange pepper,	1 teaspoon fine sea salt
thinly sliced	6 Italian-seasoned sausages
1 red pepper, thinly sliced	Dijon mustard, for serving
60 ml avocado oil or melted	(optional)

1. Preheat the air fryer to 204°C. 2. Place the onion and peppers in a large bowl. Drizzle with the oil and toss well to coat the veggies. Season with the salt. 3. Place the onion and peppers in a pie pan and cook in the air fryer for 8 minutes, stirring halfway through. Remove from the air fryer and set aside. 4. Spray the air fryer basket with avocado oil. Place the sausages in the air fryer basket and air fry for 20 minutes, or until crispy and golden brown. During the last minute or two of cooking, add the onion and peppers to the basket with the sausages to warm them through. 5. Place the onion and peppers on a serving platter and arrange the sausages on top. Serve Dijon mustard on the side, if desired. 6. Store leftovers in an airtight container in the fridge for up to 7 days or in the freezer for up to a month. Reheat in a preheated 200°C air fryer for 3 minutes, or until heated through.

Caraway Crusted Beef Steaks

Prep time: 5 minutes | Cook time: 10 minutes | Serves 4

4 beef steaks	taste
2 teaspoons caraway seeds	1 tablespoon melted butter
2 teaspoons garlic powder	80 ml almond flour
Sea salt and cayenne pepper, to	2 eggs, beaten

1. Preheat the air fryer to 179°C. 2. Add the beef steaks to a large bowl and toss with the caraway seeds, garlic powder, salt and pepper until well coated. 3. Stir together the melted butter and almond flour in a bowl. Whisk the eggs in a different bowl. 4. Dredge the seasoned steaks in the eggs, then dip in the almond and butter mixture. 5. Arrange the coated steaks in the air fryer basket. Air fryer for 10 minutes, or until the internal temperature of the beef steaks reaches at least 64°C on a meat thermometer. Flip the steaks once halfway through to ensure even cooking. 6. Transfer the steaks to plates. Let cool for 5 minutes and serve hot.

Greek Lamb Pitta Pockets

Prep time: 15 minutes | Cook time: 6 minutes | Serves 4

Dressing:	¼ teaspoon coriander
235 ml plain yogurt	¼ teaspoon ground cumin
1 tablespoon lemon juice	¼ teaspoon salt
1 teaspoon dried dill, crushed	4 pitta halves
1 teaspoon ground oregano	Suggested Toppings:
½ teaspoon salt	1 red onion, slivered
Meatballs:	1 medium cucumber, deseeded,
230 g lamb mince	thinly sliced
1 tablespoon diced onion	Crumbled feta cheese
1 teaspoon dried parsley	Sliced black olives
1 teaspoon dried dill, crushed	Chopped fresh peppers
¼ teaspoon oregano	

1. Preheat the air fryer to 200°C. 2. Stir the dressing ingredients together in a small bowl and refrigerate while preparing lamb. 3. Combine all meatball ingredients in a large bowl and stir to distribute seasonings. 4. Shape meat mixture into 12 small meatballs, rounded or slightly flattened if you prefer. 5. Transfer the meatballs in the preheated air fryer and air fry for 6 minutes, until well done. Remove and drain on paper towels. 6. To serve, pile meatballs and the choice of toppings in pitta pockets and drizzle with dressing.

Herbed Lamb Steaks

Prep time: 30 minutes | Cook time: 15 minutes | Serves 4

½ medium onion	1 teaspoon cayenne pepper
2 tablespoons minced garlic	1 teaspoon salt
2 teaspoons ground ginger	4 (170 g) boneless lamb sirloin
1 teaspoon ground cinnamon	steaks
1 teaspoon onion granules	Oil, for spraying

1. In a blender, combine the onion, garlic, ginger, cinnamon, onion granules, cayenne pepper, and salt and pulse until the onion is minced. 2. Place the lamb steaks in a large bowl or zip-top plastic bag and sprinkle the onion mixture over the top. Turn the steaks until they are evenly coated. Cover with plastic wrap or seal the bag and refrigerate for 30 minutes. 3. Preheat the air fryer to 164°C. Line the air fryer basket with parchment and spray lightly with oil. 4. Place the lamb steaks in a single layer in the prepared basket, making sure they don't overlap. You may need to work in batches, depending on the size of your air fryer. 5. Cook for 8 minutes, flip, and cook for another 7 minutes, or until the internal temperature reaches 68°C.

Spaghetti Zoodles and Meatballs

Prep time: 30 minutes | Cook time: 11 to 13 minutes | Serves 6

450 g beef mince	Freshly ground black pepper, to
1½ teaspoons sea salt, plus	taste
more for seasoning	Avocado oil spray
1 large egg, beaten	Keto-friendly marinara sauce,
1 teaspoon gelatin	for serving
180 ml Parmesan cheese	170 g courgette noodles, made
2 teaspoons minced garlic	using a spiralizer or store-
1 teaspoon Italian seasoning	bought

1. Place the beef mince in a large bowl, and season with the salt. 2. Place the egg in a separate bowl and sprinkle with the gelatin. Allow to sit for 5 minutes. 3. Stir the gelatin mixture, then pour it over the ground beef. Add the Parmesan, garlic, and Italian seasoning. Season with salt and pepper. 4. Form the mixture into 1½-inch meatballs and place them on a plate; cover with plastic wrap and refrigerate for at least 1 hour or overnight. 5. Spray the meatballs with oil. Set the air fryer to 204°C and arrange the meatballs in a single layer in the air fryer basket. Air fry for 4 minutes. Flip the meatballs and spray them with more oil. Air fry for 4 minutes more, until an instant-read thermometer reads 72°C.

Transfer the meatballs to a plate and allow them to rest. 6. While the meatballs are resting, heat the marinara in a saucepan on the stove over medium heat. 7. Place the courgette noodles in the air fryer, and cook at 204°C for 3 to 5 minutes. 8. To serve, place the courgette noodles in serving bowls. Top with meatballs and warm marinara.

Ham Hock Mac and Cheese

Prep time: 20 minutes | Cook time: 25 minutes | Serves 4

2 large eggs, beaten	1 teaspoon freshly ground black
475 ml cottage cheese, full-fat	pepper
or low-fat	475 ml uncooked elbow
475 ml grated sharp Cheddar	macaroni
cheese, divided	2 ham hocks (about 310 g
235 ml sour cream	each), meat removed and diced
½ teaspoon salt	1 to 2 tablespoons oil

1. In a large bowl, stir together the eggs, cottage cheese, 235 ml of the Cheddar cheese, sour cream, salt, and pepper. 2. Stir in the macaroni and the diced meat. 3. Preheat the air fryer to 182°C. Spritz a baking pan with oil. 4. Pour the macaroni mixture into the prepared pan, making sure all noodles are covered with sauce. 5. Cook for 12 minutes. Stir in the remaining 235 ml of Cheddar cheese, making sure all the noodles are covered with sauce. Cook for 13 minutes more, until the noodles are tender. Let rest for 5 minutes before serving.

Mediterranean Beef Steaks

Prep time: 20 minutes | Cook time: 20 minutes | Serves 4

2 tablespoons soy sauce or	pepper
tamari	½ teaspoon dried basil
3 heaping tablespoons fresh	½ teaspoon dried rosemary
chives	1 teaspoon freshly ground black
2 tablespoons olive oil	pepper
3 tablespoons dry white wine	1 teaspoon sea salt, or more to
4 small-sized beef steaks	taste
2 teaspoons smoked cayenne	

1. Firstly, coat the steaks with the cayenne pepper, black pepper, salt, basil, and rosemary. 2. Drizzle the steaks with olive oil, white wine, and soy sauce. 3. Finally, roast in the air fryer for 20 minutes at 172°C. Serve garnished with fresh chives. Bon appétit!

Kheema Meatloaf

Prep time: 10 minutes | Cook time: 15 minutes | Serves 4

450 g 85% lean beef mince	2 teaspoons garam masala
2 large eggs, lightly beaten	1 teaspoon coarse or flaky salt
235 ml diced brown onion	1 teaspoon ground turmeric
60 ml chopped fresh coriander	1 teaspoon cayenne pepper
1 tablespoon minced fresh ginger	½ teaspoon ground cinnamon
1 tablespoon minced garlic	⅛ teaspoon ground cardamom

1. In a large bowl, gently mix the beef mince, eggs, onion, coriander, ginger, garlic, garam masala, salt, turmeric, cayenne, cinnamon, and cardamom until thoroughly combined. 2. Place the seasoned meat in a baking pan. Place the pan in the air fryer basket. Set the air fryer to 176°C for 15 minutes. Use a meat thermometer to ensure the meat loaf has reached an internal temperature of 72°C (medium). 3. Drain the fat and liquid from the pan and let stand for 5 minutes before slicing. 4. Slice and serve hot.

Pork Loin with Aloha Salsa

Prep time: 20 minutes | Cook time: 7 to 9 minutes | Serves 4

Aloha Salsa:	2 eggs
235 ml fresh pineapple, chopped in small pieces	2 tablespoons milk
	60 ml flour
60 ml red onion, finely chopped	60 ml panko bread crumbs
60 ml green or red pepper, chopped	4 teaspoons sesame seeds
	450 g boneless, thin pork loin
½ teaspoon ground cinnamon	or tenderloin (⅜- to ½-inch
1 teaspoon reduced-salt soy sauce	thick)
	Pepper and salt
⅛ teaspoon crushed red pepper	60 ml cornflour
⅛ teaspoon ground black pepper	Oil for misting or cooking spray

1. In a medium bowl, stir together all ingredients for salsa. Cover and refrigerate while cooking pork. 2. Preheat the air fryer to 200°C. 3. Beat together eggs and milk in shallow dish. 4. In another shallow dish, mix together the flour, panko, and sesame seeds. 5. Sprinkle pork with pepper and salt to taste. 6. Dip pork in cornflour, egg mixture, and then panko coating. Spray both sides with oil or cooking spray. 7. Cook pork for 3 minutes. Turn pork over, spraying both sides, and continue cooking for 4 to 6 minutes or until well done. 8. Serve fried cutlets with salsa on the side.

Steak Gyro Platter

Prep time: 30 minutes | Cook time: 8 to 10 minutes | Serves 4

450 g bavette or skirt steak	120 ml peeled and diced cucumber
1 teaspoon garlic powder	
1 teaspoon ground cumin	80 ml sliced red onion
½ teaspoon sea salt	60 ml seeded and diced tomato
½ teaspoon freshly ground black pepper	2 tablespoons pitted and sliced black olives
140 g shredded romaine lettuce	Tzatziki sauce, for serving
120 ml crumbled feta cheese	

1. Pat the steak dry with paper towels. In a small bowl, combine the garlic powder, cumin, salt, and pepper. Sprinkle this mixture all over the steak, and allow the steak to rest at room temperature for 45 minutes. 2. Preheat the air fryer to 204°C. Place the steak in the air fryer basket and air fry for 4 minutes. Flip the steak and cook 4 to 6 minutes more, until an instant-read thermometer reads 49°C at the thickest point for medium-rare (or as desired). Remove the steak from the air fryer and let it rest for 5 minutes. 3. Divide the romaine among plates. Top with the feta, cucumber, red onion, tomato, and olives.

Indian Mint and Chile Kebabs

Prep time: 30 minutes | Cook time: 15 minutes | Serves 4

450 g lamb mince	½ teaspoon ground turmeric
120 ml finely minced onion	½ teaspoon cayenne pepper
60 ml chopped fresh mint	¼ teaspoon ground cardamom
60 ml chopped fresh coriander	¼ teaspoon ground cinnamon
1 tablespoon minced garlic	1 teaspoon coarse or flaky salt

1. In the bowl of a stand mixer fitted with the paddle attachment, combine the lamb, onion, mint, coriander, garlic, turmeric, cayenne, cardamom, cinnamon, and salt. Mix on low speed until you have a sticky mess of spiced meat. If you have time, let the mixture stand at room temperature for 30 minutes (or cover and refrigerate for up to a day or two, until you're ready to make the kebabs). 2. Divide the meat into eight equal portions. Form each into a long sausage shape. Place the kebabs in a single layer in the air fryer basket. Set the air fryer to 176°C for 10 minutes. Increase the air fryer temperature to 204°C and cook for 3 to 4 minutes more to brown the kebabs. Use a meat thermometer to ensure the kebabs have reached an internal temperature of 72°C (medium).

Sausage-Stuffed Peppers

Prep time: 15 minutes | Cook time: 28 to 30 minutes | Serves 6

Avocado oil spray

230 g Italian-seasoned sausage, casings removed

120 ml chopped mushrooms

60 ml diced onion

1 teaspoon Italian seasoning

Sea salt and freshly ground black pepper, to taste

235 ml keto-friendly marinara sauce

3 peppers, halved and seeded

85 g low-moisture Mozzarella or other melting cheese, shredded

1. Spray a large skillet with oil and place it over medium-high heat. Add the sausage and cook for 5 minutes, breaking up the meat with a wooden spoon. Add the mushrooms, onion, and Italian seasoning, and season with salt and pepper. Cook for 5 minutes more. Stir in the marinara sauce and cook until heated through. 2. Scoop the sausage filling into the pepper halves. 3. Set the air fryer to 176°C. Arrange the peppers in a single layer in the air fryer basket, working in batches if necessary. Air fry for 15 minutes. 4. Top the stuffed peppers with the cheese and air fry for 3 to 5 minutes more, until the cheese is melted and the peppers are tender.

Smothered Chops

Prep time: 20 minutes | Cook time: 30 minutes | Serves 4

4 bone-in pork chops (230 g each)

2 teaspoons salt, divided

1½ teaspoons freshly ground black pepper, divided

1 teaspoon garlic powder

235 ml tomato purée

1½ teaspoons Italian seasoning

1 tablespoon sugar

1 tablespoon cornflour

120 ml chopped onion

120 ml chopped green pepper

1 to 2 tablespoons oil

1. Evenly season the pork chops with 1 teaspoon salt, 1 teaspoon pepper, and the garlic powder. 2. In a medium bowl, stir together the tomato purée, Italian seasoning, sugar, remaining 1 teaspoon of salt, and remaining ½ teaspoon of pepper. 3. In a small bowl, whisk 180 ml water and the cornflour until blended. Stir this slurry into the tomato purée, with the onion and green pepper. Transfer to a baking pan. 4. Preheat the air fryer to 176°C. 5. Place the sauce in the fryer and cook for 10 minutes. Stir and cook for 10 minutes more. Remove the pan and keep warm. 6. Increase the air fryer temperature to 204°C. Line the air fryer basket with parchment paper. 7. Place the pork chops on the parchment and spritz with oil. 8. Cook for 5 minutes. Flip and spritz the chops with oil and cook for 5 minutes more, until the internal temperature reaches 64°C. Serve with the tomato mixture spooned on top.

Chapter 6 Fish and Seafood

Chapter 6 Fish and Seafood

Dukkah-Crusted Halibut

Prep time: 15 minutes | Cook time: 17 minutes | Serves 2

Dukkah:	¼ teaspoon black pepper
1 tablespoon coriander seeds	Fish:
1 tablespoon sesame seeds	2 halibut fillets, 140 g each
1½ teaspoons cumin seeds	2 tablespoons mayonnaise
50 g roasted mixed nuts	Vegetable oil spray
¼ teaspoon kosher or coarse sea salt	Lemon wedges, for serving

1. For the Dukkah: Combine the coriander, sesame seeds, and cumin in a small baking pan. Place the pan in the air fryer basket. Set the air fryer to 204ºC for 5 minutes. Toward the end of the cooking time, you will hear the seeds popping. Transfer to a plate and let cool for 5 minutes. 2. Transfer the toasted seeds to a food processor or spice grinder and add the mixed nuts. Pulse until coarsely chopped. Add the salt and pepper and stir well. 3. For the fish: Spread each fillet with 1 tablespoon of the mayonnaise. Press a heaping tablespoon of the Dukkah into the mayonnaise on each fillet, pressing lightly to adhere. 4. Spray the air fryer basket with vegetable oil spray. Place the fish in the basket. Cook for 12 minutes, or until the fish flakes easily with a fork. 5. Serve the fish with lemon wedges.

Salmon on Bed of Fennel and Carrot

Prep time: 15 minutes | Cook time: 13 to 14 minutes | Serves 2

1 fennel bulb, thinly sliced	¼ teaspoon coarsely ground pepper
1 large carrot, peeled and sliced	
1 small onion, thinly sliced	2 salmon fillets, 140 g each
60 ml low-fat sour cream	

1. Combine the fennel, carrot, and onion in a bowl and toss. 2. Put the vegetable mixture into a baking pan. Roast in the air fryer at 204ºC for 4 minutes or until the vegetables are crisp-tender. 3. Remove the pan from the air fryer. Stir in the sour cream and sprinkle the vegetables with the pepper. 4. Top with the salmon fillets. 5. Return the pan to the air fryer. Roast for another 9 to 10 minutes or until the salmon just barely flakes when tested with a fork.

Crab-Stuffed Avocado Boats

Prep time: 5 minutes | Cook time: 7 minutes | Serves 4

2 medium avocados, halved and pitted	2 tablespoons peeled and diced yellow onion
230 g cooked crab meat	2 tablespoons mayonnaise
¼ teaspoon Old Bay seasoning	

1. Scoop out avocado flesh in each avocado half, leaving ½ inch around edges to form a shell. Chop scooped-out avocado. 2. In a medium bowl, combine crab meat, Old Bay seasoning, onion, mayonnaise, and chopped avocado. Place ¼ mixture into each avocado shell. 3. Place avocado boats into ungreased air fryer basket. Adjust the temperature to 176ºC and air fry for 7 minutes. Avocado will be browned on the top and mixture will be bubbling when done. Serve warm.

Prawns with Smoky Tomato Dressing

Prep time: 5 minutes | Cook time: 8 minutes | Serves 2

3 tablespoons mayonnaise	salt
1 tablespoon ketchup	455 g large raw prawns (21 to 25 count), peeled (tails left on) and deveined
1 tablespoon minced garlic	
1 teaspoon Sriracha	
½ teaspoon smoked paprika	Vegetable oil spray
½ teaspoon kosher or coarse sea salt	50 g chopped spring onions

1. In a large bowl, combine the mayonnaise, ketchup, garlic, Sriracha, paprika, and salt. Add the prawns and toss to coat with the sauce. 2. Spray the air fryer basket with vegetable oil spray. Place the prawns in the basket. Set the air fryer to 176ºC for 8 minutes, tossing and spraying the prawns with vegetable oil spray halfway through the cooking time. 3. Sprinkle with the chopped spring onions before serving.

Blackened Fish

Prep time: 15 minutes | Cook time: 8 minutes | Serves 4

1 large egg, beaten	4 tilapia fillets, 110g each
Blackened seasoning, as needed	Cooking spray
2 tablespoons light brown sugar	

1. In a shallow bowl, place the beaten egg. In a second shallow bowl, stir together the Blackened seasoning and the brown sugar. 2. One at a time, dip the fish fillets in the egg, then the brown sugar mixture, coating thoroughly. 3. Preheat the air fryer to 150°C. Line the air fryer basket with baking paper. 4. Place the coated fish on the baking paper and spritz with oil. 5. Bake for 4 minutes. Flip the fish, spritz it with oil, and bake for 4 to 6 minutes more until the fish is white inside and flakes easily with a fork. 6. Serve immediately.

Mediterranean-Style Cod

Prep time: 5 minutes | Cook time: 12 minutes | Serves 4

4 cod fillets, 170 g each	6 cherry tomatoes, halved
3 tablespoons fresh lemon juice	45 g pitted and sliced kalamata
1 tablespoon olive oil	olives
¼ teaspoon salt	

1. Place cod into an ungreased round nonstick baking dish. Pour lemon juice into dish and drizzle cod with olive oil. Sprinkle with salt. Place tomatoes and olives around baking dish in between fillets. 2. Place dish into air fryer basket. Adjust the temperature to 176°C and bake for 12 minutes, carefully turning cod halfway through cooking. Fillets will be lightly browned, easily flake, and have an internal temperature of at least 64°C when done. Serve warm.

Sole and Asparagus Bundles

Prep time: 10 minutes | Cook time: 14 minutes | Serves 2

230 g asparagus, trimmed	softened
1 teaspoon extra-virgin olive oil, divided	1 small shallot, minced
Salt and pepper, to taste	1 tablespoon chopped fresh tarragon
4 (85 g) skinless sole fillets, ⅛ to ¼ inch thick	¼ teaspoon lemon zest plus ½ teaspoon juice
4 tablespoons unsalted butter,	Vegetable oil spray

1. Preheat the air fryer to 150°C. 2. Toss asparagus with ½ teaspoon oil, pinch salt, and pinch pepper in a bowl. Cover and microwave until bright green and just tender, about 3 minutes, tossing halfway through microwaving. Uncover and set aside to cool slightly. 3. Make foil sling for air fryer basket by folding 1 long sheet of aluminum foil so it is 4 inches wide. Lay sheet of foil widthwise across basket, pressing foil into and up sides of basket. Fold excess foil as needed so that edges of foil are flush with top of basket. Lightly spray foil and basket with vegetable oil spray. 4. Pat sole dry with paper towels and season with salt and pepper. Arrange fillets skinned side up on cutting board, with thicker ends closest to you. Arrange asparagus evenly across base of each fillet, then tightly roll fillets away from you around asparagus to form tidy bundles. 5. Rub bundles evenly with remaining ½ teaspoon oil and arrange seam side down on sling in prepared basket. Bake until asparagus is tender and sole flakes apart when gently prodded with a paring knife, 14 to 18 minutes, using a sling to rotate bundles halfway through cooking. 6. Combine butter, shallot, tarragon, and lemon zest and juice in a bowl. Using sling, carefully remove sole bundles from air fryer and transfer to individual plates. Top evenly with butter mixture and serve.

Fish Fillets with Lemon-Dill Sauce

Prep time: 5 minutes | Cook time: 7 minutes | Serves 4

455 g snapper, grouper, or salmon fillets	60 g mayonnaise
Sea salt and freshly ground black pepper, to taste	2 tablespoons fresh dill, chopped, plus more for garnish
1 tablespoon avocado oil	1 tablespoon freshly squeezed lemon juice
60 g sour cream	½ teaspoon grated lemon zest

1. Pat the fish dry with paper towels and season well with salt and pepper. Brush with the avocado oil. 2. Set the air fryer to 204°C. Place the fillets in the air fryer basket and air fry for 1 minute. 3. Lower the air fryer temperature to 164°C and continue cooking for 5 minutes. Flip the fish and cook for 1 minute more or until an instant-read thermometer reads 64°C. (If using salmon, cook it to 52°C /125°F for medium-rare.) 4. While the fish is cooking, make the sauce by combining the sour cream, mayonnaise, dill, lemon juice, and lemon zest in a medium bowl. Season with salt and pepper and stir until combined. Refrigerate until ready to serve. 5. Serve the fish with the sauce, garnished with the remaining dill.

Catfish Bites

Prep time: 15 minutes | Cook time: 20 minutes | Serves 4

Olive or vegetable oil, for spraying	70 g cornmeal
455 g catfish fillets, cut into 2-inch pieces	30 g plain flour
	2 teaspoons Creole seasoning
235 ml buttermilk	120 ml yellow mustard

1. Line the air fryer basket with baking paper and spray lightly with oil. 2. Place the catfish pieces and buttermilk in a zip-top plastic bag, seal, and refrigerate for about 10 minutes. 3. In a shallow bowl, mix together the cornmeal, flour, and Creole seasoning. 4. Remove the catfish from the bag and pat dry with a paper towel. 5. Spread the mustard on all sides of the catfish, then dip them in the cornmeal mixture until evenly coated. 6. Place the catfish in the prepared basket. You may need to work in batches, depending on the size of your air fryer. Spray lightly with oil. 7. Air fry at 204°C for 10 minutes, flip carefully, spray with oil, and cook for another 10 minutes. Serve immediately.

Nutty Prawns with Amaretto Glaze

Prep time: 30 minutes | Cook time: 10 minutes per batch | Serves 10 to 12

120 g plain flour	oil
½ teaspoon baking powder	185 g sliced almonds
1 teaspoon salt	900 g large prawns (about
2 eggs, beaten	32 to 40 prawns), peeled and
120 ml milk	deveined, tails left on
2 tablespoons olive or vegetable	470 ml amaretto liqueur

1. Combine the flour, baking powder and salt in a large bowl. Add the eggs, milk and oil and stir until it forms a smooth batter. Coarsely crush the sliced almonds into a second shallow dish with your hands. 2. Dry the prawns well with paper towels. Dip the prawns into the batter and shake off any excess batter, leaving just enough to lightly coat the prawns. Transfer the prawns to the dish with the almonds and coat completely. Place the coated prawns on a plate or baking sheet and when all the prawns have been coated, freeze the prawns for an 1 hour, or as long as a week before air frying. 3. Preheat the air fryer to 204°C. 4. Transfer 8 frozen prawns at a time to the air fryer basket. Air fry for 6 minutes. Turn the prawns over and air fry for an additional 4 minutes. Repeat with the remaining prawns. 5. While the prawns are cooking, bring the Amaretto to a boil in a small saucepan on the stovetop. Lower the heat and simmer until it has reduced and thickened into a glaze, about 10 minutes. 6. Remove the prawns from the air fryer and brush both sides with the warm amaretto glaze. Serve warm.

Tuna Melt

Prep time: 3 minutes | Cook time: 10 minutes | Serves 1

Olive or vegetable oil, for spraying	more for garnish
	2 teaspoons unsalted butte
140 g can tuna, drained	2 slices sandwich bread of
1 tablespoon mayonnaise	choice
¼ teaspoon garlic granules, plus	2 slices Cheddar cheese

1. Line the air fryer basket with baking paper and spray lightly with oil. 2. In a medium bowl, mix together the tuna, mayonnaise, and garlic. 3. Spread 1 teaspoon of butter on each slice of bread and place one slice butter-side down in the prepared basket. 4. Top with a slice of cheese, the tuna mixture, another slice of cheese, and the other slice of bread, butter-side up. 5. Air fry at 204°C for 5 minutes, flip, and cook for another 5 minutes, until browned and crispy. 6. Sprinkle with additional garlic, before cutting in half and serving.

Browned Prawns Patties

Prep time: 15 minutes | Cook time: 10 to 12 minutes | Serves 4

230 g raw prawns, peeled, deveined and chopped finely	sauce
	½ teaspoon salt
500 g cooked sushi rice	½ teaspoon garlic powder
35 g chopped red bell pepper	½ teaspoon Old Bay seasoning
35 g chopped celery	75 g plain bread crumbs
35 g chopped spring onion	Cooking spray
2 teaspoons Worcestershire	

1. Preheat the air fryer to 200°C. 2. Put all the ingredients except the bread crumbs and oil in a large bowl and stir to incorporate. 3. Scoop out the prawn mixture and shape into 8 equal-sized patties with your hands, no more than ½-inch thick. Roll the patties in the bread crumbs on a plate and spray both sides with cooking spray. 4. Place the patties in the air fryer basket. You may need to work in batches to avoid overcrowding. 5. Air fry for 10 to 12 minutes, flipping the patties halfway through, or until the outside is crispy brown. 6. Divide the patties among four plates and serve warm.

Greek Fish Pitas

Prep time: 10 minutes | Cook time: 15 minutes | Serves 4

455 g pollock, cut into 1-inch pieces	¼ teaspoon cayenne
60 ml olive oil	4 whole wheat pitas
1 teaspoon salt	75 g shredded lettuce
½ teaspoon dried oregano	2 plum tomatoes, diced
½ teaspoon dried thyme	Nonfat plain Greek yogurt
½ teaspoon garlic powder	Lemon, quartered

1. Preheat the air fryer to 192°C. 2. In a medium bowl, combine the pollock with olive oil, salt, oregano, thyme, garlic powder, and cayenne. 3. Put the pollock into the air fryer basket and roast for 15 minutes. 4. Serve inside pitas with lettuce, tomato, and Greek yogurt with a lemon wedge on the side.

Fish Sandwich with Tartar Sauce

Prep time: 10 minutes | Cook time: 17 minutes | Serves 2

Tartar Sauce:	Fish:
115 g mayonnaise	2 tablespoons plain flour
2 tablespoons onion granules	1 egg, lightly beaten
1 dill pickle spear, finely chopped	120 g panko
2 teaspoons pickle juice	2 teaspoons lemon pepper
¼ teaspoon salt	2 tilapia fillets
⅛ teaspoon ground black pepper	Cooking spray
	2 soft sub rolls

1. Preheat the air fryer to 204°C. 2. In a small bowl, combine the mayonnaise, onion granules, pickle, pickle juice, salt, and pepper. 3. Whisk to combine and chill in the refrigerator while you make the fish. 4. Place a baking paper liner in the air fryer basket. 5. Scoop the flour out onto a plate; set aside. 6. Put the beaten egg in a medium shallow bowl. 7. On another plate, mix to combine the panko and lemon pepper. 8. Dredge the tilapia fillets in the flour, then dip in the egg, and then press into the panko mixture. 9. Place the prepared fillets on the liner in the air fryer in a single layer. 10. Spray lightly with cooking spray and air fry for 8 minutes. Carefully flip the fillets, spray with more cooking spray, and air fry for an additional 9 minutes, until golden and crispy. 11. Place each cooked fillet in a sub roll, top with a little bit of tartar sauce, and serve.

Crunchy Fish Sticks

Prep time: 30 minutes | Cook time: 9 minutes | Serves 4

455 g cod fillets	black pepper, to taste
170 g finely ground blanched almond flour	60 ml mayonnaise
2 teaspoons Old Bay seasoning	1 large egg, beaten
½ teaspoon paprika	Avocado oil spray
Sea salt and freshly ground	Tartar sauce, for serving

1. Cut the fish into ¾-inch-wide strips. 2. In a shallow bowl, stir together the almond flour, Old Bay seasoning, paprika, and salt and pepper to taste. In another shallow bowl, whisk together the mayonnaise and egg. 3. Dip the cod strips in the egg mixture, then the almond flour, gently pressing with your fingers to help adhere to the coating. 4. Place the coated fish on a baking paper -lined baking sheet and freeze for 30 minutes. 5. Spray the air fryer basket with oil. Set the air fryer to 204°C. Place the fish in the basket in a single layer, and spray each piece with oil. 6. Cook for 5 minutes. Flip and spray with more oil. Cook for 4 minutes more, until the internal temperature reaches 60°C. Serve with the tartar sauce.

Almond-Crusted Fish

Prep time: 15 minutes | Cook time: 10 minutes | Serves 4

4 firm white fish fillets, 110g each	Salt and pepper, to taste
45 g breadcrumbs	940 g plain flour
20 g slivered almonds, crushed	1 egg, beaten with 1 tablespoon water
2 tablespoons lemon juice	Olive or vegetable oil for
⅛ teaspoon cayenne	misting or cooking spray

1. Split fish fillets lengthwise down the center to create 8 pieces. 2. Mix breadcrumbs and almonds together and set aside. 3. Mix the lemon juice and cayenne together. Brush on all sides of fish. 4. Season fish to taste with salt and pepper. 5. Place the flour on a sheet of wax paper. 6. Roll fillets in flour, dip in egg wash, and roll in the crumb mixture. 7. Mist both sides of fish with oil or cooking spray. 8. Spray the air fryer basket and lay fillets inside. 9. Roast at 200°C for 5 minutes, turn fish over, and cook for an additional 5 minutes or until fish is done and flakes easily.

Crab Cakes

Prep time: 10 minutes | Cook time: 10 minutes | Serves 4

2 cans lump crab meat, 170 g each	½ teaspoon Dijon mustard
¼ cup blanched finely ground almond flour	½ tablespoon lemon juice
	½ medium green bell pepper, seeded and chopped
1 large egg	235 g chopped spring onion
2 tablespoons full-fat mayonnaise	½ teaspoon Old Bay seasoning

1. In a large bowl, combine all ingredients. Form into four balls and flatten into patties. Place patties into the air fryer basket. 2. Adjust the temperature to 176°C and air fry for 10 minutes. 3. Flip patties halfway through the cooking time. Serve warm.

Tilapia with Pecans

Prep time: 20 minutes | Cook time: 16 minutes | Serves 5

2 tablespoons ground flaxseeds	2 tablespoons extra-virgin olive oil
1 teaspoon paprika	
Sea salt and white pepper, to taste	65 g pecans, ground
1 teaspoon garlic paste	5 tilapia fillets, sliced into halves

1. Combine the ground flaxseeds, paprika, salt, white pepper, garlic paste, olive oil, and ground pecans in a sealable freezer bag. Add the fish fillets and shake to coat well. 2. Spritz the air fryer basket with cooking spray. Cook in the preheated air fryer at 204°C for 10 minutes; turn them over and cook for 6 minutes more. Work in batches. 3. Serve with lemon wedges, if desired. Enjoy!

Tuna Avocado Bites

Prep time: 10 minutes | Cook time: 7 minutes |
Makes 12 bites

280 g can tuna, drained	pitted, and mashed
60 ml full-fat mayonnaise	50 g blanched finely ground almond flour, divided
1 stalk celery, chopped	
1 medium avocado, peeled,	2 teaspoons coconut oil

1. In a large bowl, mix tuna, mayonnaise, celery, and mashed avocado. Form the mixture into balls. 2. Roll balls in almond flour and spritz with coconut oil. Place balls into the air fryer basket. 3. Adjust the temperature to 204°C and set the timer for 7 minutes. 4. Gently turn tuna bites after 5 minutes. Serve warm.

Tandoori Prawns

Prep time: 25 minutes | Cook time: 6 minutes | Serves 4

455 g jumbo raw prawns (21 to 25 count), peeled and deveined	1 teaspoon garam masala
	1 teaspoon smoked paprika
1 tablespoon minced fresh ginger	1 teaspoon kosher or coarse sea salt
3 cloves garlic, minced	½ to 1 teaspoon cayenne pepper
5 g chopped fresh coriander or parsley, plus more for garnish	2 tablespoons olive oil (for Paleo) or melted ghee
1 teaspoon ground turmeric	2 teaspoons fresh lemon juice

1. In a large bowl, combine the prawns, ginger, garlic, coriander, turmeric, garam masala, paprika, salt, and cayenne. Toss well to coat. Add the oil or ghee and toss again. Marinate at room temperature for 15 minutes, or cover and refrigerate for up to 8 hours. 2. Place the prawns in a single layer in the air fryer basket. Set the air fryer to 164°C for 6 minutes. Transfer the prawns to a serving platter. Cover and let the prawns finish cooking in the residual heat, about 5 minutes. 3. Sprinkle the prawns with the lemon juice and toss to coat. Garnish with additional cilantro and serve.

Prawns Pasta with Basil and Mushrooms

Prep time: 10 minutes | Cook time: 10 minutes | Serves 6

455 g small prawns, peeled and deveined	5 garlic cloves, minced
	230 g baby mushrooms, sliced
120 ml olive oil plus 1 tablespoon, divided	45 g Parmesan, plus more for serving (optional)
¼ teaspoon garlic powder	1 teaspoon salt
¼ teaspoon cayenne	½ teaspoon black pepper
455 g whole grain pasta	½ cup fresh basil

1. Preheat the air fryer to 192°C. 2. In a small bowl, combine the prawns, 1 tablespoon olive oil, garlic powder, and cayenne. Toss to coat the prawns. 3. Place the prawns into the air fryer basket and roast for 5 minutes. Remove the prawns and set aside. 4. Cook the pasta according to package directions. Once done cooking, reserve ½ cup pasta water, then drain. 5. Meanwhile, in a large skillet, heat 120 ml of olive oil over medium heat. Add the garlic and mushrooms and cook down for 5 minutes. 6. Pour the pasta, reserved pasta water, Parmesan, salt, pepper, and basil into the skillet with the vegetable-and-oil mixture, and stir to coat the pasta. 7. Toss in the prawns and remove from heat, then let the mixture sit for 5 minutes before serving with additional Parmesan, if desired.

Scallops in Lemon-Butter Sauce

Prep time: 10 minutes | Cook time: 6 minutes | Serves 2

8 large dry sea scallops (about 340 g)	2 tablespoons chopped flat-leaf parsley
Salt and freshly ground black pepper, to taste	1 tablespoon fresh lemon juice
2 tablespoons olive oil	2 teaspoons capers, drained and chopped
2 tablespoons unsalted butter, melted	1 teaspoon grated lemon zest
	1 clove garlic, minced

1. Preheat the air fryer to 204°C. 2. Use a paper towel to pat the scallops dry. Sprinkle lightly with salt and pepper. Brush with the olive oil. Arrange the scallops in a single layer in the air fryer basket. Pausing halfway through the cooking time to turn the scallops, air fry for about 6 minutes until firm and opaque. 3. Meanwhile, in a small bowl, combine the oil, butter, parsley, lemon juice, capers, lemon zest, and garlic. Drizzle over the scallops just before serving.

Lemon Pepper Prawns

Prep time: 15 minutes | Cook time: 8 minutes | Serves 2

Olive or vegetable oil, for spraying	1 tablespoon olive oil
340 g medium raw prawns, peeled and deveined	1 teaspoon lemon pepper
	¼ teaspoon paprika
3 tablespoons lemon juice	¼ teaspoon granulated garlic

1. Preheat the air fryer to 204°C. Line the air fryer basket with baking paper and spray lightly with oil. 2. In a medium bowl, toss together the prawns, lemon juice, olive oil, lemon pepper, paprika, and garlic until evenly coated. 3. Place the prawns in the prepared basket. 4. Cook for 6 to 8 minutes, or until pink and firm. Serve immediately.

Air Fryer Fish Fry

Prep time: 5 minutes | Cook time: 15 minutes | Serves 4

470 ml low-fat buttermilk	70 g plain yellow cornmeal
½ teaspoon garlic powder	45 g chickpea flour
½ teaspoon onion powder	¼ teaspoon cayenne pepper
4 (110 g) sole fillets	Freshly ground black pepper

1. In a large bowl, combine the buttermilk, garlic powder, and onion powder. 2. Add the sole, turning until well coated, and set aside to marinate for 20 minutes. 3. In a shallow bowl, stir the cornmeal, chickpea flour, cayenne, and pepper together. 4. Dredge the fillets in the meal mixture, turning until well coated. Place in the basket of an air fryer. 5. Set the air fryer to 192°C, close, and cook for 12 minutes.

Miso Salmon

Prep time: 10 minutes | Cook time: 12 minutes | Serves 2

2 tablespoons brown sugar	black pepper
2 tablespoons soy sauce	2 salmon fillets, 140 g each
2 tablespoons white miso paste	Vegetable oil spray
1 teaspoon minced garlic	1 teaspoon sesame seeds
1 teaspoon minced fresh ginger	2 spring onions, thinly sliced, for garnish
½ teaspoon freshly cracked	

1. In a small bowl, whisk together the brown sugar, soy sauce, miso, garlic, ginger, and pepper to combine. 2. Place the salmon fillets on a plate. Pour half the sauce over the fillets; turn the fillets to coat the other sides with sauce. 3. Spray the air fryer basket with vegetable oil spray. Place the sauce-covered salmon in the basket. Set the air fryer to 204°C for 12 minutes. Halfway through the cooking time, brush additional miso sauce on the salmon. 4. Sprinkle the salmon with the sesame seeds and spring onions and serve.

Cajun Catfish Cakes with Cheese

Prep time: 5 minutes | Cook time: 35 minutes | Serves 4

2 catfish fillets	120 ml buttermilk
85 g butter	1 teaspoon baking powder
150 g shredded Parmesan cheese	1 teaspoon baking soda
150 g shredded Swiss cheese	1 teaspoon Cajun seasoning

1. Bring a pot of salted water to a boil. Add the catfish fillets to the boiling water and let them boil for 5 minutes until they become opaque. 2. Remove the fillets from the pot to a mixing bowl and flake them into small pieces with a fork. 3. Add the remaining ingredients to the bowl of fish and stir until well incorporated. 4. Divide the fish mixture into 12 equal portions and shape each portion into a patty. 5. Preheat the air fryer to 192°C. 6. Arrange the patties in the air fryer basket and air fry in batches for 15 minutes until golden brown and cooked through. Flip the patties halfway through the cooking time. 7. Let the patties sit for 5 minutes and serve.

Chilean Sea Bass with Olive Relish

Prep time: 10 minutes | Cook time: 10 minutes | Serves 2

Olive oil spray

2 (170 g) Chilean sea bass fillets or other firm-fleshed white fish

3 tablespoons extra-virgin olive oil

½ teaspoon ground cumin

½ teaspoon kosher or coarse sea salt

½ teaspoon black pepper

60 g pitted green olives, diced

10 g finely diced onion

1 teaspoon chopped capers

1. Spray the air fryer basket with the olive oil spray. Drizzle the fillets with the olive oil and sprinkle with the cumin, salt, and pepper. Place the fish in the air fryer basket. Set the air fryer to 164ºC for 10 minutes, or until the fish flakes easily with a fork. 2. Meanwhile, in a small bowl, stir together the olives, onion, and capers. 3. Serve the fish topped with the relish.

Chapter 7 Snacks and Appetizers

Chapter 7 Snacks and Appetizers

Easy Spiced Nuts

Prep time: 5 minutes | Cook time: 25 minutes | Makes 3 L

1 egg white, lightly beaten	¼ teaspoon ground allspice
60 ml sugar	Pinch ground cayenne pepper
1 teaspoon salt	240 ml pecan halves
½ teaspoon ground cinnamon	240 ml cashews
¼ teaspoon ground cloves	240 ml almonds

1. Combine the egg white with the sugar and spices in a bowl. 2. Preheat the air fryer to 148°C. 3. Spray or brush the air fryer basket with vegetable oil. Toss the nuts together in the spiced egg white and transfer the nuts to the air fryer basket. 4. Air fry for 25 minutes, stirring the nuts in the basket a few times during the cooking process. Taste the nuts (carefully because they will be very hot) to see if they are crunchy and nicely toasted. Air fry for a few more minutes if necessary. 5. Serve warm or cool to room temperature and store in an airtight container for up to two weeks.

Courgette Fries with Roasted Garlic Aioli

Prep time: 20 minutes | Cook time: 12 minutes | Serves 4

1 tablespoon vegetable oil	Courgette Fries:
½ head green or savoy cabbage, finely shredded	120 ml flour
	2 eggs, beaten
Roasted Garlic Aioli:	240 ml seasoned breadcrumbs
1 teaspoon roasted garlic	Salt and pepper, to taste
120 ml mayonnaise	1 large courgette, cut into
2 tablespoons olive oil	½-inch sticks
Juice of ½ lemon	Olive oil
Salt and pepper, to taste	

1. Make the aioli: Combine the roasted garlic, mayonnaise, olive oil and lemon juice in a bowl and whisk well. Season the aioli with salt and pepper to taste. 2. Prepare the courgette fries. Create a dredging station with three shallow dishes. Place the flour in the first shallow dish and season well with salt and freshly ground black pepper. Put the beaten eggs in the second shallow dish. In the third shallow dish, combine the breadcrumbs, salt and pepper. Dredge the courgette sticks, coating with flour first, then dipping them into the eggs to coat, and finally tossing in breadcrumbs. Shake the dish with the breadcrumbs and pat the crumbs onto the courgette sticks gently with your hands, so they stick evenly. 3. Place the courgette fries on a flat surface and let them sit at least 10 minutes before air frying to let them dry out a little. Preheat the air fryer to 204°C. 4. Spray the courgette sticks with olive oil and place them into the air fryer basket. You can air fry the courgette in two layers, placing the second layer in the opposite direction to the first. Air fry for 12 minutes turning and rotating the fries halfway through the cooking time. Spray with additional oil when you turn them over. 5. Serve courgette fries warm with the roasted garlic aioli.

Crispy Green Bean Fries with Lemon-Yoghurt Sauce

Prep time: 5 minutes | Cook time: 5 minutes | Serves 4

Green Beans:	227 g whole green beans
1 egg	Lemon-Yoghurt Sauce:
2 tablespoons water	120 ml non-fat plain Greek
1 tablespoon wholemeal flour	yoghurt
¼ teaspoon paprika	1 tablespoon lemon juice
½ teaspoon garlic powder	¼ teaspoon salt
½ teaspoon salt	⅛ teaspoon cayenne pepper
60 ml wholemeal breadcrumbs	

Make the Green Beans: 1. Preheat the air fryer to 192°C. 2. In a medium shallow bowl, beat together the egg and water until frothy. 3. In a separate medium shallow bowl, whisk together the flour, paprika, garlic powder, and salt, then mix in the breadcrumbs. 4. Spray the bottom of the air fryer with cooking spray. 5. Dip each green bean into the egg mixture, then into the bread crumb mixture, coating the outside with the crumbs. Place the green beans in a single layer in the bottom of the air fryer basket. 6. Fry in the air fryer for 5 minutes, or until the breading is golden brown. Make the Lemon-Yoghurt Sauce: 7. In a small bowl, combine the yoghurt, lemon juice, salt, and cayenne. 8. Serve the green bean fries alongside the lemon-yoghurt sauce as a snack or appetizer.

Stuffed Fried Mushrooms

Prep time: 20 minutes | Cook time: 10 to 11 minutes | Serves 10

120 ml panko breadcrumbs	1 (227 g) package soft white
½ teaspoon freshly ground	cheese, at room temperature
black pepper	20 cremini or button
½ teaspoon onion powder	mushrooms, stemmed
½ teaspoon cayenne pepper	1 to 2 tablespoons oil

1. In a medium bowl, whisk the breadcrumbs, black pepper, onion powder, and cayenne until blended. 2. Add the soft white cheese and mix until well blended. Fill each mushroom top with 1 teaspoon of the soft white cheese mixture 3. Preheat the air fryer to 182ºC. Line the air fryer basket with a piece of parchment paper. 4. Place the mushrooms on the parchment and spritz with oil. 5. Cook for 5 minutes. Shake the basket and cook for 5 to 6 minutes more until the filling is firm and the mushrooms are soft.

Italian Rice Balls

Prep time: 20 minutes | Cook time: 10 minutes | Makes 8 rice balls

355 ml cooked sticky rice	into tiny pieces (small enough
½ teaspoon Italian seasoning	to stuff into olives)
blend	2 eggs
¾ teaspoon salt, divided	80 ml Italian breadcrumbs
8 black olives, pitted	177 ml panko breadcrumbs
28 g Mozzarella cheese, cut	Cooking spray

1. Preheat air fryer to 200ºC. 2. Stuff each black olive with a piece of Mozzarella cheese. Set aside. 3. In a bowl, combine the cooked sticky rice, Italian seasoning blend, and ½ teaspoon of salt and stir to mix well. Form the rice mixture into a log with your hands and divide it into 8 equal portions. Mould each portion around a black olive and roll into a ball. 4. Transfer to the freezer to chill for 10 to 15 minutes until firm. 5. In a shallow dish, place the Italian breadcrumbs. In a separate shallow dish, whisk the eggs. In a third shallow dish, combine the panko breadcrumbs and remaining salt. 6. One by one, roll the rice balls in the Italian breadcrumbs, then dip in the whisked eggs, finally coat them with the panko breadcrumbs. 7. Arrange the rice balls in the air fryer basket and spritz both sides with cooking spray. 8. Air fry for 10 minutes until the rice balls are golden brown. Flip the balls halfway through the cooking time. 9. Serve warm.

Pickle Chips

Prep time: 30 minutes | Cook time: 12 minutes | Serves 4

Oil, for spraying	475 ml plain flour
475 ml sliced dill or sweet	2 large eggs, beaten
pickles, drained	475 ml panko breadcrumbs
240 ml buttermilk	¼ teaspoon salt

1. Line the air fryer basket with parchment and spray lightly with oil. 2. In a shallow bowl, combine the pickles and buttermilk and let soak for at least 1 hour, then drain. 3. Place the flour, beaten eggs, and breadcrumbs in separate bowls. 4. Coat each pickle chip lightly in the flour, dip in the eggs, and dredge in the breadcrumbs. Be sure each one is evenly coated. 5. Place the pickle chips in the prepared basket, sprinkle with the salt, and spray lightly with oil. You may need to work in batches, depending on the size of your air fryer. 6. Air fry at 200ºC for 5 minutes, flip, and cook for another 5 to 7 minutes, or until crispy. Serve hot.

Lemon Shrimp with Garlic Olive Oil

Prep time: 5 minutes | Cook time: 6 minutes | Serves 4

454 g medium shrimp, cleaned	½ teaspoon salt
and deveined	¼ teaspoon red pepper flakes
60 ml plus 2 tablespoons olive	Lemon wedges, for serving
oil, divided	(optional)
Juice of ½ lemon	Marinara sauce, for dipping
3 garlic cloves, minced and	(optional)
divided	

1. Preheat the air fryer to 192ºC. 2. In a large bowl, combine the shrimp with 2 tablespoons of the olive oil, as well as the lemon juice, ⅓ of the minced garlic, salt, and red pepper flakes. Toss to coat the shrimp well. 3. In a small ramekin, combine the remaining 60 ml of olive oil and the remaining minced garlic. 4. Tear off a 12-by-12-inch sheet of aluminium foil. Pour the shrimp into the centre of the foil, then fold the sides up and crimp the edges so that it forms an aluminium foil bowl that is open on top. Place this packet into the air fryer basket. 5. Roast the shrimp for 4 minutes, then open the air fryer and place the ramekin with oil and garlic in the basket beside the shrimp packet. Cook for 2 more minutes. 6. Transfer the shrimp on a serving plate or platter with the ramekin of garlic olive oil on the side for dipping. You may also serve with lemon wedges and marinara sauce, if desired.

Crunchy Tex-Mex Tortilla Chips

Prep time: 5 minutes | Cook time: 5 minutes | Serves 4

Olive oil	½ teaspoon paprika
½ teaspoon salt	Pinch cayenne pepper
½ teaspoon ground cumin	8 (6-inch) corn tortillas, each
½ teaspoon chilli powder	cut into 6 wedges

1. Spray fryer basket lightly with olive oil. 2. In a small bowl, combine the salt, cumin, chilli powder, paprika, and cayenne pepper. 3. Place the tortilla wedges in the air fryer basket in a single layer. Spray the tortillas lightly with oil and sprinkle with some of the seasoning mixture. You will need to cook the tortillas in batches. 4. Air fry at 192ºC for 2 to 3 minutes. Shake the basket and cook until the chips are light brown and crispy, an additional 2 to 3 minutes. Watch the chips closely so they do not burn.

Pork and Cabbage Egg Rolls

**Prep time: 15 minutes | Cook time: 12 minutes |
Makes 12 egg rolls**

Cooking oil spray	ginger
2 garlic cloves, minced	475 ml shredded green cabbage
340 g minced pork	4 spring onions, green parts
1 teaspoon sesame oil	(white parts optional), chopped
60 ml soy sauce	24 egg roll wrappers
2 teaspoons grated peeled fresh	

1. Spray a skillet with the cooking oil and place it over medium-high heat. Add the garlic and cook for 1 minute until fragrant. 2. Add the minced pork to the skillet. Using a spoon, break the pork into smaller chunks. 3. In a small bowl, whisk the sesame oil, soy sauce, and ginger until combined. Add the sauce to the skillet. Stir to combine and continue cooking for about 5 minutes until the pork is browned and thoroughly cooked. 4. Stir in the cabbage and spring onions. Transfer the pork mixture to a large bowl. 5. Lay the egg roll wrappers on a flat surface. Dip a basting brush in water and glaze each egg roll wrapper along the edges with the wet brush. This will soften the dough and make it easier to roll. 6. Stack 2 egg roll wrappers (it works best if you double-wrap the egg rolls). Scoop 1 to 2 tablespoons of the pork mixture into the centre of each wrapper stack. 7. Roll one long side of the wrappers up over the filling. Press firmly on the area with the filling, tucking it in lightly to secure it in place. Fold in the left and right sides. Continue rolling to close. Use the basting brush to wet the seam and seal the egg roll. Repeat with the remaining ingredients. 8. Insert the crisper plate into the basket and the basket into the unit. Preheat the unit by selecting AIR FRY, setting the temperature to 204ºC, and setting the time to 3 minutes. Select START/STOP to begin. 9. Once the unit is preheated, spray the crisper plate with cooking oil. Place the egg rolls into the basket. It is okay to stack them. Spray them with cooking oil. 10. Select AIR FRY, set the temperature to 204ºC, and set the time to 12 minutes. Insert the basket into the unit. Select START/STOP to begin. 11. After 8 minutes, use tongs to flip the egg rolls. Reinsert the basket to resume cooking. 12. When the cooking is complete, serve the egg rolls hot.

Greek Yoghurt Devilled Eggs

Prep time: 15 minutes | Cook time: 15 minutes | Serves 4

4 eggs	⅛ teaspoon paprika
60 ml non-fat plain Greek	⅛ teaspoon garlic powder
yoghurt	Chopped fresh parsley, for
1 teaspoon chopped fresh dill	garnish
⅛ teaspoon salt	

1. Preheat the air fryer to 127ºC. 2. Place the eggs in a single layer in the air fryer basket and cook for 15 minutes. 3. Quickly remove the eggs from the air fryer and place them into a cold water bath. Let the eggs cool in the water for 10 minutes before removing and peeling them. 4. After peeling the eggs, cut them in half. 5. Spoon the yolk into a small bowl. Add the yoghurt, dill, salt, paprika, and garlic powder and mix until smooth. 6. Spoon or pipe the yolk mixture into the halved egg whites. Serve with a sprinkle of fresh parsley on top.

Easy Roasted Chickpeas

**Prep time: 5 minutes | Cook time: 15 minutes |
Makes about 240 ml**

1 (425 g) can chickpeas,	¼ teaspoon salt
drained	1 tablespoon olive oil
2 teaspoons curry powder	

1. Drain chickpeas thoroughly and spread in a single layer on paper towels. Cover with another paper towel and press gently to remove extra moisture. Don't press too hard or you'll crush the chickpeas. 2. Mix curry powder and salt together. 3. Place chickpeas in a medium bowl and sprinkle with seasonings. Stir well to coat. 4. Add olive oil and stir again to distribute oil. 5. Air fry at 200ºC for 15 minutes, stopping to shake basket about halfway through cooking time. 6. Cool completely and store in airtight container.

Sausage Balls with Cheese

Prep time: 10 minutes | Cook time: 10 to 11 minutes

| Serves 8

340 g mild sausage meat	85 g soft white cheese, at room
355 ml baking mix	temperature
240 ml shredded mild Cheddar	1 to 2 tablespoons olive oil
cheese	

1. Preheat the air fryer to 164°C. Line the air fryer basket with parchment paper. 2. Mix together the ground sausage, baking mix, Cheddar cheese, and soft white cheese in a large bowl and stir to incorporate. 3. Divide the sausage mixture into 16 equal portions and roll them into 1-inch balls with your hands. 4. Arrange the sausage balls on the parchment, leaving space between each ball. You may need to work in batches to avoid overcrowding. 5. Brush the sausage balls with the olive oil. Bake for 10 to 11 minutes, shaking the basket halfway through, or until the balls are firm and lightly browned on both sides. 6. Remove from the basket to a plate and repeat with the remaining balls. 7. Serve warm.

Classic Spring Rolls

Prep time: 10 minutes | Cook time: 9 minutes |

Makes 16 spring rolls

4 teaspoons toasted sesame oil	240 ml grated carrot
6 medium garlic cloves, minced	½ teaspoon sea salt
or pressed	16 rice paper wrappers
1 tablespoon grated peeled	Cooking oil spray (sunflower,
fresh ginger	safflower, or refined coconut)
475 ml thinly sliced shiitake	Gluten-free sweet and sour
mushrooms	sauce or Thai sweet chilli sauce,
1 L chopped green cabbage	for serving (optional)

1. Place a wok or sauté pan over medium heat until hot. 2. Add the sesame oil, garlic, ginger, mushrooms, cabbage, carrot, and salt. Cook for 3 to 4 minutes, stirring often, until the cabbage is lightly wilted. Remove the pan from the heat. 3. Gently run a rice paper under water. Lay it on a flat non-absorbent surface. Place about 60 ml of the cabbage filling in the middle. Once the wrapper is soft enough to roll, fold the bottom up over the filling, fold in the sides, and roll the wrapper all the way up. (Basically, make a tiny burrito.) 4. Repeat step 3 to make the remaining spring rolls until you have the number of spring rolls you want to cook right now (and the amount that will fit in the air fryer basket in a single layer without them touching each other). Refrigerate any leftover filling in an airtight container for about 1 week. 5. Insert the crisper plate into the basket and the basket into the unit. Preheat the unit by selecting AIR FRY, setting the temperature to 200°C, and setting the time to 3 minutes. Select START/STOP to begin. 6. Once the unit is preheated, spray the crisper plate and the basket with cooking oil. Place the spring rolls into the basket, leaving a little room between them so they don't stick to each other. Spray the top of each spring roll with cooking oil. 7. Select AIR FRY, set the temperature to 200°C, and set the time to 9 minutes. Select START/STOP to begin. 8. When the cooking is complete, the egg rolls should be crisp-ish and lightly browned. Serve immediately, plain or with a sauce of choice.

Poutine with Waffle Fries

Prep time: 10 minutes | Cook time: 15 to 17 minutes

| Serves 4

475 ml frozen waffle cut fries	2 spring onions, sliced
2 teaspoons olive oil	240 ml shredded Swiss cheese
1 red pepper, chopped	120 ml bottled chicken gravy

1. Preheat the air fryer to 192°C. 2. Toss the waffle fries with the olive oil and place in the air fryer basket. Air fry for 10 to 12 minutes, or until the fries are crisp and light golden brown, shaking the basket halfway through the cooking time. 3. Transfer the fries to a baking pan and top with the pepper, spring onions, and cheese. Air fry for 3 minutes, or until the vegetables are crisp and tender. 4. Remove the pan from the air fryer and drizzle the gravy over the fries. Air fry for 2 minutes, or until the gravy is hot. 5. Serve immediately.

Roasted Mushrooms with Garlic

Prep time: 3 minutes | Cook time: 22 to 27 minutes |

Serves 4

16 garlic cloves, peeled	⅛ teaspoon freshly ground
2 teaspoons olive oil, divided	black pepper
16 button mushrooms	1 tablespoon white wine or low-
½ teaspoon dried marjoram	salt vegetable broth

1. In a baking pan, mix the garlic with 1 teaspoon of olive oil. Roast in the air fryer at 176°C for 12 minutes. 2. Add the mushrooms, marjoram, and pepper. Stir to coat. Drizzle with the remaining 1 teaspoon of olive oil and the white wine. 3. Return to the air fryer and roast for 10 to 15 minutes more, or until the mushrooms and garlic cloves are tender. Serve.

Crispy Breaded Beef Cubes

Prep time: 10 minutes | Cook time: 12 to 16 minutes | Serves 4

450 g sirloin tip, cut into 1-inch cubes	355 ml soft breadcrumbs
	2 tablespoons olive oil
240 ml cheese pasta sauce	½ teaspoon dried marjoram

1. Preheat the air fryer to 182ºC. 2. In a medium bowl, toss the beef with the pasta sauce to coat. 3. In a shallow bowl, combine the breadcrumbs, oil, and marjoram, and mix well. Drop the beef cubes, one at a time, into the bread crumb mixture to coat thoroughly. 4. Air fry the beef in two batches for 6 to 8 minutes, shaking the basket once during cooking time, until the beef is at least 63ºC and the outside is crisp and brown. 5. Serve hot.

Garlic-Roasted Tomatoes and Olives

Prep time: 5 minutes | Cook time: 20 minutes | Serves 6

475 ml cherry tomatoes	1 tablespoon fresh basil, minced
4 garlic cloves, roughly chopped	1 tablespoon fresh oregano, minced
½ red onion, roughly chopped	2 tablespoons olive oil
240 ml black olives	¼ to ½ teaspoon salt
240 ml green olives	

1. Preheat the air fryer to 192ºC. 2. In a large bowl, combine all of the ingredients and toss together so that the tomatoes and olives are coated well with the olive oil and herbs. 3. Pour the mixture into the air fryer basket, and roast for 10 minutes. Stir the mixture well, then continue roasting for an additional 10 minutes. 4. Remove from the air fryer, transfer to a serving bowl, and enjoy.

Bacon-Wrapped Pickle Spears

Prep time: 10 minutes | Cook time: 8 minutes | Serves 4

8 to 12 slices bacon	cheese
60 ml soft white cheese	8 dill pickle spears
60 ml shredded Mozzarella	120 ml ranch dressing

1. Lay the bacon slices on a flat surface. In a medium bowl, combine the soft white cheese and Mozzarella. Stir until well blended. Spread the cheese mixture over the bacon slices. 2. Place a pickle spear on a bacon slice and roll the bacon around the pickle in a spiral, ensuring the pickle is fully covered. (You may need to use more than one slice of bacon per pickle to fully cover the spear.) Tuck in the ends to ensure the bacon stays put. Repeat to wrap all the pickles. 3. Place the wrapped pickles in the air fryer basket in a single layer. Set the air fryer to 204ºC for 8 minutes, or until the bacon is cooked through and crisp on the edges. 4. Serve the pickle spears with ranch dressing on the side.

Black Bean Corn Dip

Prep time: 10 minutes | Cook time: 10 minutes | Serves 4

½ (425 g) can black beans, drained and rinsed	60 ml shredded low-fat Cheddar cheese
½ (425 g) can corn, drained and rinsed	½ teaspoon ground cumin
	½ teaspoon paprika
60 ml chunky salsa	Salt and freshly ground black pepper, to taste
57 g low-fat soft white cheese	

1. Preheat the air fryer to 164ºC. 2. In a medium bowl, mix together the black beans, corn, salsa, soft white cheese, Cheddar cheese, cumin, and paprika. Season with salt and pepper and stir until well combined. 3. Spoon the mixture into a baking dish. 4. Place baking dish in the air fryer basket and bake until heated through, about 10 minutes. 5. Serve hot.

Courgette Feta Roulades

Prep time: 10 minutes | Cook time: 10 minutes | Serves 6

120 ml feta	⅛ teaspoon salt
1 garlic clove, minced	⅛ teaspoon red pepper flakes
2 tablespoons fresh basil, minced	1 tablespoon lemon juice
	2 medium courgette
1 tablespoon capers, minced	12 toothpicks

1. Preheat the air fryer to 182ºC. (If using a grill attachment, make sure it is inside the air fryer during preheating.) 2. In a small bowl, combine the feta, garlic, basil, capers, salt, red pepper flakes, and lemon juice. 3. Slice the courgette into ⅛-inch strips lengthwise. (Each courgette should yield around 6 strips.) 4. Spread 1 tablespoon of the cheese filling onto each slice of courgette, then roll it up and secure it with a toothpick through the middle. 5. Place the courgette roulades into the air fryer basket in a single layer, making sure that they don't touch each other. 6. Bake or grill in the air fryer for 10 minutes. 7. Remove the courgette roulades from the air fryer and gently remove the toothpicks before serving.

Kale Chips with Tex-Mex Dip

Prep time: 10 minutes | Cook time: 5 to 6 minutes |
Serves 8

240 ml Greek yoghurt

1 tablespoon chilli powder

80 ml low-salt salsa, well drained

1 bunch curly kale

1 teaspoon olive oil

¼ teaspoon coarse sea salt

1. In a small bowl, combine the yoghurt, chilli powder, and drained salsa; refrigerate. 2. Rinse the kale thoroughly, and pat dry. Remove the stems and ribs from the kale, using a sharp knife. Cut or tear the leaves into 3-inch pieces. 3. Toss the kale with the olive oil in a large bowl. 4. Air fry the kale in small batches at 200ºC until the leaves are crisp. This should take 5 to 6 minutes. Shake the basket once during cooking time. 5. As you remove the kale chips, sprinkle them with a bit of the sea salt. 6. When all of the kale chips are done, serve with the dip.

Sweet Potato Fries with Mayonnaise

Prep time: 5 minutes | Cook time: 20 minutes |
Serves 2 to 3

1 large sweet potato (about 450 g), scrubbed

1 teaspoon vegetable or rapeseed oil

Salt, to taste

Dipping Sauce:

60 ml light mayonnaise

½ teaspoon sriracha sauce

1 tablespoon spicy brown mustard

1 tablespoon sweet Thai chilli sauce

1. Preheat the air fryer to 92ºC. 2. On a flat work surface, cut the sweet potato into fry-shaped strips about ¼ inch wide and ¼ inch thick. You can use a mandoline to slice the sweet potato quickly and uniformly. 3. In a medium bowl, drizzle the sweet potato strips with the oil and toss well. 4. Transfer to the air fryer basket and air fry for 10 minutes, shaking the basket twice during cooking. 5. Remove the air fryer basket and sprinkle with the salt and toss to coat. 6. Increase the air fryer temperature to 204ºC and air fry for an additional 10 minutes, or until the fries are crispy and tender. Shake the basket a few times during cooking. 7. Meanwhile, whisk together all the ingredients for the sauce in a small bowl. 8. Remove the sweet potato fries from the basket to a plate and serve warm alongside the dipping sauce.

Rumaki

Prep time: 30 minutes | Cook time: 10 to 12 minutes
per batch | Makes about 24 rumaki

283 g raw chicken livers

1 can sliced water chestnuts, drained

60 ml low-salt teriyaki sauce

12 slices turkey bacon

1. Cut livers into 1½-inch pieces, trimming out tough veins as you slice. 2. Place livers, water chestnuts, and teriyaki sauce in small container with lid. If needed, add another tablespoon of teriyaki sauce to make sure livers are covered. Refrigerate for 1 hour. 3. When ready to cook, cut bacon slices in half crosswise. 4. Wrap 1 piece of liver and 1 slice of water chestnut in each bacon strip. Secure with toothpick. 5. When you have wrapped half of the livers, place them in the air fryer basket in a single layer. 6. Air fry at 200ºC for 10 to 12 minutes, until liver is done, and bacon is crispy. 7. While first batch cooks, wrap the remaining livers. Repeat step 6 to cook your second batch.

Fried Artichoke Hearts

Prep time: 10 minutes | Cook time: 12 minutes |
Serves 10

Oil, for spraying

3 (397 g) cans quartered artichokes, drained and patted dry

120 ml mayonnaise

240 ml panko breadcrumbs

80 ml grated Parmesan cheese

Salt and freshly ground black pepper, to taste

1. Line the air fryer basket with parchment and spray lightly with oil. 2. Place the artichokes on a plate. Put the mayonnaise and breadcrumbs in separate bowls. 3. Working one at a time, dredge each artichoke piece in the mayonnaise, then in the breadcrumbs to cover. 4. Place the artichokes in the prepared basket. You may need to work in batches, depending on the size of your air fryer. 5. Air fry at 188ºC for 10 to 12 minutes, or until crispy and golden brown. 6. Sprinkle with the Parmesan cheese and season with salt and black pepper. Serve immediately.

Root Veggie Chips with Herb Salt

Prep time: 10 minutes | Cook time: 8 minutes | Serves 2

1 parsnip, washed

1 small beetroot, washed

1 small turnip, washed

½ small sweet potato, washed

1 teaspoon olive oil

Cooking spray

Herb Salt:

¼ teaspoon rock salt

2 teaspoons finely chopped fresh parsley

1. Preheat the air fryer to 182ºC. 2. Peel and thinly slice the parsnip, beetroot, turnip, and sweet potato, then place the vegetables in a large bowl, add the olive oil, and toss. 3. Spray the air fryer basket with cooking spray, then place the vegetables in the basket and air fry for 8 minutes, gently shaking the basket halfway through. 4. While the chips cook, make the herb salt in a small bowl by combining the rock salt and parsley. 5. Remove the chips and place on a serving plate, then sprinkle the herb salt on top and allow to cool for 2 to 3 minutes before serving.

Old Bay Chicken Wings

Prep time: 10 minutes | Cook time: 12 to 15 minutes | Serves 4

2 tablespoons Old Bay or all-purpose seasoning

2 teaspoons baking powder

2 teaspoons salt

900 g chicken wings, patted dry

Cooking spray

1. Preheat the air fryer to 204ºC. Lightly spray the air fryer basket with cooking spray. 2. Combine the seasoning, baking powder, and salt in a large zip-top plastic bag. Add the chicken wings, seal, and shake until the wings are thoroughly coated in the seasoning mixture. 3. Lay the chicken wings in the air fryer basket in a single layer and lightly mist with cooking spray. You may need to work in batches to avoid overcrowding. 4. Air fry for 12 to 15 minutes, flipping the wings halfway through, or until the wings are lightly browned and the internal temperature reaches at least 74ºC on a meat thermometer. 5. Remove from the basket to a plate and repeat with the remaining chicken wings. 6. Serve hot.

Tortellini with Spicy Dipping Sauce

Prep time: 5 minutes | Cook time: 20 minutes | Serves 4

177 ml mayonnaise

2 tablespoons mustard

1 egg

120 ml flour

½ teaspoon dried oregano

355 ml breadcrumbs

2 tablespoons olive oil

475 ml frozen cheese tortellini

1. Preheat the air fryer to 192ºC. 2. In a small bowl, combine the mayonnaise and mustard and mix well. Set aside. 3. In a shallow bowl, beat the egg. In a separate bowl, combine the flour and oregano. In another bowl, combine the breadcrumbs and olive oil, and mix well. 4. Drop the tortellini, a few at a time, into the egg, then into the flour, then into the egg again, and then into the breadcrumbs to coat. Put into the air fryer basket, cooking in batches. 5. Air fry for about 10 minutes, shaking halfway through the cooking time, or until the tortellini are crisp and golden brown on the outside. Serve with the mayonnaise mixture.

Chapter 8 Vegetables and Sides

Chapter 8 Vegetables and Sides

Sausage-Stuffed Mushroom Caps

Prep time: 10 minutes | Cook time: 8 minutes | Serves 2

6 large portobello mushroom caps	2 tablespoons blanched finely ground almond flour
230 g Italian sausage	20 g grated Parmesan cheese
15 g chopped onion	1 teaspoon minced fresh garlic

1. Use a spoon to hollow out each mushroom cap, reserving scrapings. 2. In a medium skillet over medium heat, brown the sausage about 10 minutes or until fully cooked and no pink remains. Drain and then add reserved mushroom scrapings, onion, almond flour, Parmesan, and garlic. Gently fold ingredients together and continue cooking an additional minute, then remove from heat. 3. Evenly spoon the mixture into mushroom caps and place the caps into a 6-inch round pan. Place pan into the air fryer basket. 4. Adjust the temperature to 192ºC and set the timer for 8 minutes. 5. When finished cooking, the tops will be browned and bubbling. Serve warm.

Caesar Whole Cauliflower

Prep time: 20 minutes | Cook time: 30 minutes | Serves 2 to 4

3 tablespoons olive oil	drained and finely minced
2 tablespoons red wine vinegar	coarse sea salt and freshly
2 tablespoons Worcestershire sauce	ground black pepper, to taste
2 tablespoons grated Parmesan cheese	1 small head cauliflower (about 450 g), green leaves trimmed and stem trimmed flush with
1 tablespoon Dijon mustard	the bottom of the head
4 garlic cloves, minced	1 tablespoon roughly chopped
4 oil-packed anchovy fillets,	fresh flat-leaf parsley (optional)

1. In a liquid measuring jug, whisk together the olive oil, vinegar, Worcestershire, Parmesan, mustard, garlic, anchovies, and salt and pepper to taste. Place the cauliflower head upside down on a cutting board and use a paring knife to make an "x" through the full length of the core. Transfer the cauliflower head to a large bowl and pour half the dressing over it. Turn the cauliflower head to coat it in the dressing, then let it rest, stem-side up, in the dressing for at least 10 minutes and up to 30 minutes to allow the dressing to seep into all its nooks and crannies. 2. Transfer the cauliflower head, stem-side down, to the air fryer and air fry at 170ºC or 25 minutes. Drizzle the remaining dressing over the cauliflower and air fry at 200ºC until the top of the cauliflower is golden brown and the core is tender, about 5 minutes more. 3. Remove the basket from the air fryer and transfer the cauliflower to a large plate. Sprinkle with the parsley, if you like, and serve hot.

Corn and Coriander Salad

Prep time: 10 minutes | Cook time: 10 minutes | Serves 2

2 ears of corn, shucked (halved crosswise if too large to fit in your air fryer)	coriander leaves
	1 tablespoon sour cream
1 tablespoon unsalted butter, at room temperature	1 tablespoon mayonnaise
1 teaspoon chili powder	1 teaspoon adobo sauce (from a can of chipotle peppers in
¼ teaspoon garlic powder	adobo sauce)
coarse sea salt and freshly ground black pepper, to taste	2 tablespoons crumbled feta cheese
20 g lightly packed fresh	Lime wedges, for serving

1. Brush the corn all over with the butter, then sprinkle with the chili powder and garlic powder, and season with salt and pepper. Place the corn in the air fryer and air fry at 200ºC, turning over halfway through, until the kernels are lightly charred and tender, about 10 minutes. 2. Transfer the ears to a cutting board, let stand 1 minute, then carefully cut the kernels off the cobs and move them to a bowl. Add the coriander leaves and toss to combine (the coriander leaves will wilt slightly). 3. In a small bowl, stir together the sour cream, mayonnaise, and adobo sauce. Divide the corn and coriander among plates and spoon the adobo dressing over the top. Sprinkle with the feta cheese and serve with lime wedges on the side.

Mashed Sweet Potato Tots

Prep time: 10 minutes | Cook time: 12 to 13 minutes per batch | Makes 18 to 24 tots

210 g cooked mashed sweet potatoes	2 tablespoons chopped pecans
1 egg white, beaten	1½ teaspoons honey
⅛ teaspoon ground cinnamon	Salt, to taste
1 dash nutmeg	50 g panko bread crumbs
	Oil for misting or cooking spray

1. Preheat the air fryer to 200°C. 2. In a large bowl, mix together the potatoes, egg white, cinnamon, nutmeg, pecans, honey, and salt to taste. 3. Place panko crumbs on a sheet of wax paper. 4. For each tot, use about 2 teaspoons of sweet potato mixture. To shape, drop the measure of potato mixture onto panko crumbs and push crumbs up and around potatoes to coat edges. Then turn tot over to coat other side with crumbs. 5. Mist tots with oil or cooking spray and place in air fryer basket in single layer. 6. Air fry at 200°C for 12 to 13 minutes, until browned and crispy. 7. Repeat steps 5 and 6 to cook remaining tots.

Blackened Courgette with Kimchi-Herb Sauce

Prep time: 10 minutes | Cook time: 15 minutes | Serves 2

2 medium courgettes, ends trimmed (about 170 g each)	garnish
2 tablespoons olive oil	2 tablespoons rice vinegar
75 g kimchi, finely chopped	2 teaspoons Asian chili-garlic sauce
5 g finely chopped fresh coriander	1 teaspoon grated fresh ginger
5 g finely chopped fresh flat-leaf parsley, plus more for	coarse sea salt and freshly ground black pepper, to taste

1. Brush the courgettes with half of the olive oil, place in the air fryer, and air fry at 200°C, turning halfway through, until lightly charred on the outside and tender, about 15 minutes. 2. Meanwhile, in a small bowl, combine the remaining 1 tablespoon olive oil, the kimchi, coriander, parsley, vinegar, chili-garlic sauce, and ginger. 3. Once the courgette is finished cooking, transfer it to a colander and let it cool for 5 minutes. Using your fingers, pinch and break the courgette into bite-size pieces, letting them fall back into the colander. Season the courgette with salt and pepper, toss to combine, then let sit a further 5 minutes to allow some of its liquid to drain. Pile the courgette atop the kimchi sauce on a plate and sprinkle with more parsley to serve.

Lemon-Thyme Asparagus

Prep time: 5 minutes | Cook time: 4 to 8 minutes | Serves 4

450 g asparagus, woody ends trimmed off	Sea salt and freshly ground black pepper, to taste
1 tablespoon avocado oil	60 g goat cheese, crumbled
½ teaspoon dried thyme or ½ tablespoon chopped fresh thyme	Zest and juice of 1 lemon
	Flaky sea salt, for serving (optional)

1. In a medium bowl, toss together the asparagus, avocado oil, and thyme, and season with sea salt and pepper. 2. Place the asparagus in the air fryer basket in a single layer. Set the air fryer to 200°C and air fry for 4 to 8 minutes, to your desired doneness. 3. Transfer to a serving platter. Top with the goat cheese, lemon zest, and lemon juice. If desired, season with a pinch of flaky salt.

Parmesan Herb Focaccia Bread

Prep time: 10 minutes | Cook time: 10 minutes | Serves 6

225 g shredded Mozzarella cheese	½ teaspoon bicarbonate of soda
30 g) full-fat cream cheese	2 large eggs
95 g blanched finely ground almond flour	½ teaspoon garlic powder
40 g ground golden flaxseed	¼ teaspoon dried basil
20 g grated Parmesan cheese	¼ teaspoon dried rosemary
	2 tablespoons salted butter, melted and divided

1. Place Mozzarella, cream cheese, and almond flour into a large microwave-safe bowl and microwave for 1 minute. Add the flaxseed, Parmesan, and bicarbonate of soda and stir until smooth ball forms. If the mixture cools too much, it will be hard to mix. Return to microwave for 10 to 15 seconds to rewarm if necessary. 2. Stir in eggs. You may need to use your hands to get them fully incorporated. Just keep stirring and they will absorb into the dough. 3. Sprinkle dough with garlic powder, basil, and rosemary and knead into dough. Grease a baking pan with 1 tablespoon melted butter. Press the dough evenly into the pan. Place pan into the air fryer basket. 4. Adjust the temperature to 200°C and bake for 10 minutes. 5. At 7 minutes, cover with foil if bread begins to get too dark. 6. Remove and let cool at least 30 minutes. Drizzle with remaining butter and serve.

Crispy Chickpeas

Prep time: 5 minutes | Cook time: 15 minutes | Serves 4

1 (425 g) can chickpeas, drained but not rinsed	1 teaspoon salt
2 tablespoons olive oil	2 tablespoons lemon juice

1. Preheat the air fryer to 200°C. 2. Add all the ingredients together in a bowl and mix. Transfer this mixture to the air fryer basket. 3. Air fry for 15 minutes, ensuring the chickpeas become nice and crispy. 4. Serve immediately.

Mediterranean Courgette Boats

Prep time: 5 minutes | Cook time: 10 minutes | Serves 4

1 large courgette, ends removed, halved lengthwise	65 g feta cheese
6 grape tomatoes, quartered	1 tablespoon balsamic vinegar
¼ teaspoon salt	1 tablespoon olive oil

1. Use a spoon to scoop out 2 tablespoons from centre of each courgette half, making just enough space to fill with tomatoes and feta. 2. Place tomatoes evenly in centres of courgette halves and sprinkle with salt. Place into ungreased air fryer basket. Adjust the temperature to 180°C and roast for 10 minutes. When done, courgette will be tender. 3. Transfer boats to a serving tray and sprinkle with feta, then drizzle with vinegar and olive oil. Serve warm.

Lush Vegetable Salad

Prep time: 15 minutes | Cook time: 10 minutes | Serves 4

6 plum tomatoes, halved	oil
2 large red onions, sliced	1 teaspoon paprika
4 long red pepper, sliced	½ lemon, juiced
2 yellow pepper, sliced	Salt and ground black pepper,
6 cloves garlic, crushed	to taste
1 tablespoon extra-virgin olive	1 tablespoon baby capers

1. Preheat the air fryer to 220°C. 2. Put the tomatoes, onions, peppers, and garlic in a large bowl and cover with the extra-virgin olive oil, paprika, and lemon juice. Sprinkle with salt and pepper as desired. 3. Line the inside of the air fryer basket with aluminum foil. Put the vegetables inside and air fry for 10 minutes, ensuring the edges turn brown. 4. Serve in a salad bowl with the baby capers.

Cauliflower Rice Balls

Prep time: 10 minutes | Cook time: 8 minutes | Serves 4

1 (280 g) steamer bag cauliflower rice, cooked according to package instructions	1 large egg
	60 g plain pork scratchings, finely crushed
	¼ teaspoon salt
110 g shredded Mozzarella cheese	½ teaspoon Italian seasoning

1. Place cauliflower into a large bowl and mix with Mozzarella. 2. Whisk egg in a separate medium bowl. Place pork scratchings into another large bowl with salt and Italian seasoning. 3. Separate cauliflower mixture into four equal sections and form each into a ball. Carefully dip a ball into whisked egg, then roll in pork scratchings. Repeat with remaining balls. 4. Place cauliflower balls into ungreased air fryer basket. Adjust the temperature to 200°C and air fry for 8 minutes. Rice balls will be golden when done. 5. Use a spatula to carefully move cauliflower balls to a large dish for serving. Serve warm.

Broccoli-Cheddar Twice-Baked Potatoes

Prep time: 10 minutes | Cook time: 46 minutes | Serves 4

Oil, for spraying	1 tablespoon sour cream
2 medium Maris Piper potatoes	1 teaspoon garlic powder
1 tablespoon olive oil	1 teaspoon onion powder
30 g broccoli florets	60 g shredded Cheddar cheese

1. Line the air fryer basket with parchment and spray lightly with oil. 2. Rinse the potatoes and pat dry with paper towels. Rub the outside of the potatoes with the olive oil and place them in the prepared basket. 3. Air fry at 200°C for 40 minutes, or until easily pierced with a fork. Let cool just enough to handle, then cut the potatoes in half lengthwise. 4. Meanwhile, place the broccoli in a microwave-safe bowl, cover with water, and microwave on high for 5 to 8 minutes. Drain and set aside. 5. Scoop out most of the potato flesh and transfer to a medium bowl. 6. Add the sour cream, garlic, and onion powder and stir until the potatoes are mashed. 7. Spoon the potato mixture back into the hollowed potato skins, mounding it to fit, if necessary. Top with the broccoli and cheese. Return the potatoes to the basket. You may need to work in batches, depending on the size of your air fryer. 8. Air fry at 200°C for 3 to 6 minutes, or until the cheese has melted. Serve immediately.

Cauliflower with Lime Juice

Prep time: 10 minutes | Cook time: 7 minutes | Serves 4

215 g chopped cauliflower florets	½ teaspoon garlic powder
2 tablespoons coconut oil, melted	1 medium lime
2 teaspoons chili powder	2 tablespoons chopped coriander

1. In a large bowl, toss cauliflower with coconut oil. Sprinkle with chili powder and garlic powder. Place seasoned cauliflower into the air fryer basket. 2. Adjust the temperature to 180°C and set the timer for 7 minutes. 3. Cauliflower will be tender and begin to turn golden at the edges. Place into a serving bowl. 4. Cut the lime into quarters and squeeze juice over cauliflower. Garnish with coriander.

Parmesan and Herb Sweet Potatoes

Prep time: 10 minutes | Cook time: 18 minutes | Serves 4

2 large sweet potatoes, peeled and cubed	½ teaspoon salt
65 ml olive oil	2 tablespoons shredded Parmesan
1 teaspoon dried rosemary	

1. Preheat the air fryer to 180°C. 2. In a large bowl, toss the sweet potatoes with the olive oil, rosemary, and salt. 3. Pour the potatoes into the air fryer basket and roast for 10 minutes, then stir the potatoes and sprinkle the Parmesan over the top. Continue roasting for 8 minutes more. 4. Serve hot and enjoy.

Mole-Braised Cauliflower

Prep time: 10 minutes | Cook time: 15 minutes | Serves 2

230 g medium cauliflower florets	peanuts
1 tablespoon vegetable oil	1 tablespoon toasted sesame seeds, plus more for garnish
coarse sea salt and freshly ground black pepper, to taste	1 tablespoon finely chopped golden raisins
350 ml vegetable stock	1 teaspoon coarse sea salt
2 tablespoons New Mexico chili powder (or regular chili powder)	1 teaspoon dark brown sugar
	½ teaspoon dried oregano
	¼ teaspoon cayenne pepper
2 tablespoons salted roasted	⅛ teaspoon ground cinnamon

1. In a large bowl, toss the cauliflower with the oil and season with salt and black pepper. Transfer to a cake pan. Place the pan in the air fryer and roast at 192°C until the cauliflower is tender and lightly browned at the edges, about 10 minutes, stirring halfway through. 2. Meanwhile, in a small blender, combine the stock, chili powder, peanuts, sesame seeds, raisins, salt, brown sugar, oregano, cayenne, and cinnamon and purée until smooth. Pour into a small saucepan or skillet and bring to a simmer over medium heat, then cook until reduced by half, 3 to 5 minutes. 3. Pour the hot mole sauce over the cauliflower in the pan, stir to coat, then cook until the sauce is thickened and lightly charred on the cauliflower, about 5 minutes more. Sprinkle with more sesame seeds and serve warm.

Zesty Fried Asparagus

Prep time: 3 minutes | Cook time: 10 minutes | Serves 4

Oil, for spraying	1 tablespoon garlic powder
10 to 12 spears asparagus, trimmed	1 teaspoon chili powder
	½ teaspoon ground cumin
2 tablespoons olive oil	¼ teaspoon salt

1. Line the air fryer basket with parchment and spray lightly with oil. 2. If the asparagus are too long to fit easily in the air fryer, cut them in half. 3. Place the asparagus, olive oil, garlic, chili powder, cumin, and salt in a zip-top plastic bag, seal, and toss until evenly coated. 4. Place the asparagus in the prepared basket. 5. Roast at 200°C for 5 minutes, flip, and cook for another 5 minutes, or until bright green and firm but tender.

Marinara Pepperoni Mushroom Pizza

Prep time: 5 minutes | Cook time: 18 minutes | Serves 4

4 large portobello mushrooms, stems removed	225 g shredded Mozzarella cheese
4 teaspoons olive oil	10 slices sugar-free pepperoni
225 g marinara sauce	

1. Preheat the air fryer to 192°C. 2. Brush each mushroom cap with the olive oil, one teaspoon for each cap. 3. Put on a baking sheet and bake, stem-side down, for 8 minutes. 4. Take out of the air fryer and divide the marinara sauce, Mozzarella cheese and pepperoni evenly among the caps. 5. Air fry for another 10 minutes until browned. 6. Serve hot.

Spiced Honey-Walnut Carrots

Prep time: 5 minutes | Cook time: 12 minutes | Serves 6

450 g baby carrots	¼ teaspoon ground cinnamon
2 tablespoons olive oil	25 g black walnuts, chopped
80 g raw honey	

1. Preheat the air fryer to 180ºC. 2. In a large bowl, toss the baby carrots with olive oil, honey, and cinnamon until well coated. 3. Pour into the air fryer and roast for 6 minutes. Shake the basket, sprinkle the walnuts on top, and roast for 6 minutes more. 4. Remove the carrots from the air fryer and serve.

Courgette Balls

Prep time: 5 minutes | Cook time: 10 minutes | Serves 4

4 courgettes	1 tablespoon Italian herbs
1 egg	75 g grated coconut
45 g grated Parmesan cheese	

1. Thinly grate the courgettes and dry with a cheesecloth, ensuring to remove all the moisture. 2. In a bowl, combine the courgettes with the egg, Parmesan, Italian herbs, and grated coconut, mixing well to incorporate everything. Using the hands, mold the mixture into balls. 3. Preheat the air fryer to 200ºC. 4. Lay the courgette balls in the air fryer basket and air fry for 10 minutes. 5. Serve hot.

Spinach and Cheese Stuffed Tomatoes

Prep time: 20 minutes | Cook time: 15 minutes | Serves 2

4 ripe beefsteak tomatoes	1 (150 g) package garlic-and-
¾ teaspoon black pepper	herb Boursin cheese
½ teaspoon coarse sea salt	3 tablespoons sour cream
1 (280 g) package frozen	45 g finely grated Parmesan
chopped spinach, thawed and	cheese
squeezed dry	

1. Cut the tops off the tomatoes. Using a small spoon, carefully remove and discard the pulp. Season the insides with ½ teaspoon of the black pepper and ¼ teaspoon of the salt. Invert the tomatoes onto paper towels and allow to drain while you make the filling. 2. Meanwhile, in a medium bowl, combine the spinach, Boursin cheese, sour cream, ½ of the Parmesan, and the remaining ¼ teaspoon salt and ¼ teaspoon pepper. Stir until ingredients are well combined. Divide the filling among the tomatoes. Top with the

remaining ½ of the Parmesan. 3. Place the tomatoes in the air fryer basket. Set the air fryer to 180ºC for 15 minutes, or until the filling is hot.

Five-Spice Roasted Sweet Potatoes

Prep time: 10 minutes | Cook time: 12 minutes | Serves 4

½ teaspoon ground cinnamon	Freshly ground black pepper, to
¼ teaspoon ground cumin	taste
¼ teaspoon paprika	2 large sweet potatoes, peeled
1 teaspoon chili powder	and cut into ¾-inch cubes
⅛ teaspoon turmeric	1 tablespoon olive oil
½ teaspoon salt (optional)	

1. In a large bowl, mix together cinnamon, cumin, paprika, chili powder, turmeric, salt, and pepper to taste. 2. Add potatoes and stir well. 3. Drizzle the seasoned potatoes with the olive oil and stir until evenly coated. 4. Place seasoned potatoes in a baking pan or an ovenproof dish that fits inside your air fryer basket. 5. Cook for 6 minutes at 200ºC, stop, and stir well. 6. Cook for an additional 6 minutes.

Lemon-Garlic Mushrooms

Prep time: 10 minutes | Cook time: 10 to 15 minutes | Serves 6

340 g sliced mushrooms	1 teaspoon freshly squeezed
1 tablespoon avocado oil	lemon juice
Sea salt and freshly ground	½ teaspoon red pepper flakes
black pepper, to taste	2 tablespoons chopped fresh
3 tablespoons unsalted butter	parsley
1 teaspoon minced garlic	

1. Place the mushrooms in a medium bowl and toss with the oil. Season to taste with salt and pepper. 2. Place the mushrooms in a single layer in the air fryer basket. Set your air fryer to 192ºC and roast for 10 to 15 minutes, until the mushrooms are tender. 3. While the mushrooms cook, melt the butter in a small pot or skillet over medium-low heat. Stir in the garlic and cook for 30 seconds. Remove the pot from the heat and stir in the lemon juice and red pepper flakes. 4. Toss the mushrooms with the lemon-garlic butter and garnish with the parsley before serving.

Balsamic Brussels Sprouts

Prep time: 5 minutes | Cook time: 12 minutes | Serves 4

180 g trimmed and halved fresh Brussels sprouts	pepper
2 tablespoons olive oil	2 tablespoons balsamic vinegar
¼ teaspoon salt	2 slices cooked sugar-free bacon, crumbled
¼ teaspoon ground black	

1. In a large bowl, toss Brussels sprouts in olive oil, then sprinkle with salt and pepper. Place into ungreased air fryer basket. Adjust the temperature to 192°C and set the timer for 12 minutes, shaking the basket halfway through cooking. Brussels sprouts will be tender and browned when done. 2. Place sprouts in a large serving dish and drizzle with balsamic vinegar. Sprinkle bacon over top. Serve warm.

Fried Brussels Sprouts

Prep time: 10 minutes | Cook time: 18 minutes | Serves 4

1 teaspoon plus 1 tablespoon extra-virgin olive oil, divided	2 tablespoons sriracha
2 teaspoons minced garlic	450 g Brussels sprouts, stems trimmed and any tough leaves removed, rinsed, halved lengthwise, and dried
2 tablespoons honey	
1 tablespoon sugar	
2 tablespoons freshly squeezed lemon juice	½ teaspoon salt
2 tablespoons rice vinegar	Cooking oil spray

1. In a small saucepan over low heat, combine 1 teaspoon of olive oil, the garlic, honey, sugar, lemon juice, vinegar, and sriracha. Cook for 2 to 3 minutes, or until slightly thickened. Remove the pan from the heat, cover, and set aside. 2. Place the Brussels sprouts in a resealable bag or small bowl. Add the remaining olive oil and the salt, and toss to coat. 3. Insert the crisper plate into the basket and the basket into the unit. Preheat the unit by selecting AIR FRY, setting the temperature to 200°C, and setting the time to 3 minutes. Select START/STOP to begin. 4. Once the unit is preheated, spray the crisper plate with cooking oil. Add the Brussels sprouts to the basket. 5. Select AIR FRY, set the temperature to 200°C, and set the time to 15 minutes. Select START/STOP to begin. 6. After 7 or 8 minutes, remove the basket and shake it to toss the sprouts. Reinsert the basket to resume cooking. 7. When the cooking is complete, the leaves should be crispy and light brown and the sprout centres tender. 8. Place the sprouts in a medium serving bowl and drizzle the sauce over the top. Toss to coat, and serve immediately.

Baked Jalapeño and Cheese Cauliflower Mash

Prep time: 10 minutes | Cook time: 15 minutes | Serves 6

1 (340 g) steamer bag cauliflower florets, cooked according to package instructions	120 g shredded sharp Cheddar cheese
	20 g pickled jalapeños
2 tablespoons salted butter, softened	½ teaspoon salt
	¼ teaspoon ground black pepper
60 g cream cheese, softened	

1. Place cooked cauliflower into a food processor with remaining ingredients. Pulse twenty times until cauliflower is smooth and all ingredients are combined. 2. Spoon mash into an ungreased round nonstick baking dish. Place dish into air fryer basket. Adjust the temperature to 192°C and bake for 15 minutes. The top will be golden brown when done. Serve warm.

Gold Artichoke Hearts

Prep time: 15 minutes | Cook time: 8 minutes | Serves 4

12 whole artichoke hearts packed in water, drained	40 g panko bread crumbs
60 g plain flour	1 teaspoon Italian seasoning
1 egg	Cooking oil spray

1. Squeeze any excess water from the artichoke hearts and place them on paper towels to dry. 2. Place the flour in a small bowl. 3. In another small bowl, beat the egg. 4. In a third small bowl, stir together the panko and Italian seasoning. 5. Dip the artichoke hearts in the flour, in the egg, and into the panko mixture until coated. 6. Insert the crisper plate into the basket and the basket into the unit. Preheat the unit by selecting AIR FRY, setting the temperature to 192°C, and setting the time to 3 minutes. Select START/STOP to begin. 7. Once the unit is preheated, spray the crisper plate and the basket with cooking oil. Place the breaded artichoke hearts into the basket, stacking them if needed. 8. Select AIR FRY, set the temperature to 192°C, and set the time to 8 minutes. Select START/STOP to begin. 9. After 4 minutes, use tongs to flip the artichoke hearts. I recommend flipping instead of shaking because the hearts are small, and this will help keep the breading intact. Re-insert the basket to resume cooking. 10. When the cooking is complete, the artichoke hearts should be deep golden brown and crisp. Cool for 5 minutes before serving.

Citrus-Roasted Broccoli Florets

Prep time: 5 minutes | Cook time: 12 minutes | Serves 6

285 g broccoli florets (approximately 1 large head)

2 tablespoons olive oil

½ teaspoon salt

130 ml orange juice

1 tablespoon raw honey

Orange wedges, for serving (optional)

1. Preheat the air fryer to 180°C. 2. In a large bowl, combine the broccoli, olive oil, salt, orange juice, and honey. Toss the broccoli in the liquid until well coated. 3. Pour the broccoli mixture into the air fryer basket and roast for 6 minutes. Stir and roast for 6 minutes more. 4. Serve alone or with orange wedges for additional citrus flavour, if desired.

Chapter 9 Vegetarian Mains

Chapter 9 Vegetarian Mains

Broccoli with Garlic Sauce

Prep time: 19 minutes | Cook time: 15 minutes | Serves 4

2 tablespoons olive oil	crushed
Rock salt and freshly ground	3 garlic cloves, minced
black pepper, to taste	⅓ teaspoon dried marjoram,
450 g broccoli florets	crushed
Dipping Sauce:	60 ml sour cream
2 teaspoons dried rosemary,	80 ml mayonnaise

Lightly grease your broccoli with a thin layer of olive oil. Season with salt and ground black pepper. Arrange the seasoned broccoli in the air fryer basket. Bake at 202ºC for 15 minutes, shaking once or twice. In the meantime, prepare the dipping sauce by mixing all the sauce ingredients. Serve warm broccoli with the dipping sauce and enjoy!

Cauliflower Steak with Gremolata

Prep time: 15 minutes | Cook time: 25 minutes | Serves 4

2 tablespoons olive oil	60 ml Parmesan cheese
1 tablespoon Italian seasoning	Gremolata:
1 large head cauliflower, outer	1 bunch Italian parsley
leaves removed and sliced	2 cloves garlic
lengthwise through the core	Zest of 1 small lemon, plus 1 to
into thick "steaks"	2 teaspoons lemon juice
Salt and freshly ground black	120 ml olive oil
pepper, to taste	Salt and pepper, to taste

Preheat the air fryer to 204ºC. In a small bowl, combine the olive oil and Italian seasoning. Brush both sides of each cauliflower "steak" generously with the oil. Season to taste with salt and black pepper. Working in batches if necessary, arrange the cauliflower in a single layer in the air fryer basket. Pausing halfway through the cooking time to turn the "steaks," air fry for 15 to 20 minutes until the cauliflower is tender and the edges begin to brown. Sprinkle with the Parmesan and air fry for 5 minutes longer. To make the gremolata: In a food processor fitted with a metal blade, combine the parsley, garlic, and lemon zest and juice. With the motor running, add the olive oil in a steady stream until the mixture forms a bright green sauce. Season to taste with salt and black pepper. Serve the cauliflower steaks with the gremolata spooned over the top.

Tangy Asparagus and Broccoli

Prep time: 25 minutes | Cook time: 22 minutes | Serves 4

230 g asparagus, cut into 1½-inch pieces	Salt and white pepper, to taste
	120 ml vegetable broth
230 g broccoli, cut into 1½-inch pieces	2 tablespoons apple cider vinegar
2 tablespoons olive oil	

Place the vegetables in a single layer in the lightly greased air fryer basket. Drizzle the olive oil over the vegetables. Sprinkle with salt and white pepper. Cook at 192ºC for 15 minutes, shaking the basket halfway through the cooking time. Add 120 ml of vegetable broth to a saucepan; bring to a rapid boil and add the vinegar. Cook for 5 to 7 minutes or until the sauce has reduced by half. Spoon the sauce over the warm vegetables and serve immediately. Bon appétit!

Roasted Vegetables with Rice

Prep time: 5 minutes | Cook time: 12 minutes | Serves 4

2 teaspoons melted butter	1 red onion, chopped
235 ml chopped mushrooms	1 garlic clove, minced
235 ml cooked rice	Salt and black pepper, to taste
235 ml peas	2 hard-boiled eggs, grated
1 carrot, chopped	1 tablespoon soy sauce

Preheat the air fryer to 192ºC. Coat a baking dish with melted butter. Stir together the mushrooms, cooked rice, peas, carrot, onion, garlic, salt, and pepper in a large bowl until well mixed. Pour the mixture into the prepared baking dish and transfer to the air fryer basket. Roast in the preheated air fryer for 12 minutes until the vegetables are tender. Divide the mixture among four plates. Serve warm with a sprinkle of grated eggs and a drizzle of soy sauce.

Whole Roasted Lemon Cauliflower

Prep time: 5 minutes | Cook time: 15 minutes | Serves 4

1 medium head cauliflower	1 medium lemon
2 tablespoons salted butter, melted	½ teaspoon garlic powder
	1 teaspoon dried parsley

Remove the leaves from the head of cauliflower and brush it with melted butter. Cut the lemon in half and zest one half onto the cauliflower. Squeeze the juice of the zested lemon half and pour it over the cauliflower. Sprinkle with garlic powder and parsley. Place cauliflower head into the air fryer basket. Adjust the temperature to 176°C and air fry for 15 minutes. Check cauliflower every 5 minutes to avoid overcooking. It should be fork tender. To serve, squeeze juice from other lemon half over cauliflower. Serve immediately.

Aubergine and Courgette Bites

Prep time: 30 minutes | Cook time: 30 minutes | Serves 8

2 teaspoons fresh mint leaves, chopped	450 g aubergine, peeled and cubed
1½ teaspoons red pepper chilli flakes	450 g courgette, peeled and cubed
2 tablespoons melted butter	3 tablespoons olive oil

Toss all the above ingredients in a large-sized mixing dish. Roast the aubergine and courgette bites for 30 minutes at 164°C in your air fryer, turning once or twice. Serve with a homemade dipping sauce.

Loaded Cauliflower Steak

Prep time: 5 minutes | Cook time: 7 minutes | Serves 4

1 medium head cauliflower	melted
60 ml hot sauce	60 ml blue cheese, crumbled
2 tablespoons salted butter,	60 ml full-fat ranch dressing

Remove cauliflower leaves. Slice the head in ½-inch-thick slices. In a small bowl, mix hot sauce and butter. Brush the mixture over the cauliflower. Place each cauliflower steak into the air fryer, working in batches if necessary. Adjust the temperature to 204°C and air fry for 7 minutes. When cooked, edges will begin turning dark and caramelized. To serve, sprinkle steaks with crumbled blue cheese. Drizzle with ranch dressing.

Baked Turnip and Courgette

Prep time: 5 minutes | Cook time: 15 to 20 minutes | Serves 4

3 turnips, sliced	2 cloves garlic, crushed
1 large courgette, sliced	1 tablespoon olive oil
1 large red onion, cut into rings	Salt and black pepper, to taste

Preheat the air fryer to 166°C. Put the turnips, courgette, red onion, and garlic in a baking pan. Drizzle the olive oil over the top and sprinkle with the salt and pepper. Place the baking pan in the preheated air fryer and bake for 15 to 20 minutes, or until the vegetables are tender. Remove from the basket and serve on a plate.

Mediterranean Air Fried Veggies

Prep time: 10 minutes | Cook time: 6 minutes | Serves 4

1 large courgette, sliced	1 teaspoon mustard
235 ml cherry tomatoes, halved	1 teaspoon garlic purée
1 parsnip, sliced	6 tablespoons olive oil
1 green pepper, sliced	Salt and ground black pepper, to taste
1 carrot, sliced	to taste
1 teaspoon mixed herbs	

Preheat the air fryer to 204°C. Combine all the ingredients in a bowl, making sure to coat the vegetables well. Transfer to the air fryer and air fry for 6 minutes, ensuring the vegetables are tender and browned. Serve immediately.

Italian Baked Egg and Veggies

Prep time: 10 minutes | Cook time: 10 minutes | Serves 2

2 tablespoons salted butter	1 medium plum tomato, diced
1 small courgette, sliced lengthwise and quartered	2 large eggs
½ medium green pepper, seeded and diced	¼ teaspoon onion powder
235 ml fresh spinach, chopped	¼ teaspoon garlic powder
	½ teaspoon dried basil
	¼ teaspoon dried oregano

Grease two ramekins with 1 tablespoon butter each. In a large bowl, toss courgette, pepper, spinach, and tomato. Divide the mixture in two and place half in each ramekin. Crack an egg on top of each ramekin and sprinkle with onion powder, garlic powder, basil, and oregano. Place into the air fryer basket. Adjust the temperature to 166°C and bake for 10 minutes. Serve immediately.

Broccoli Crust Pizza

Prep time: 15 minutes | Cook time: 12 minutes | Serves 4

700 ml riced broccoli, steamed and drained well

1 large egg

120 ml grated vegetarian Parmesan cheese

3 tablespoons low-carb Alfredo sauce

120 ml shredded Mozzarella cheese

In a large bowl, mix broccoli, egg, and Parmesan. Cut a piece of parchment to fit your air fryer basket. Press out the pizza mixture to fit on the parchment, working in two batches if necessary. Place into the air fryer basket. Adjust the temperature to 188°C and air fry for 5 minutes. The crust should be firm enough to flip. If not, add 2 additional minutes. Flip crust. Top with Alfredo sauce and Mozzarella. Return to the air fryer basket and cook an additional 7 minutes or until cheese is golden and bubbling. Serve warm.

Three-Cheese Courgette Boats

Prep time: 15 minutes | Cook time: 20 minutes | Serves 2

2 medium courgette

1 tablespoon avocado oil

60 ml low-carb, no-sugar-added pasta sauce

60 ml full-fat ricotta cheese

60 ml shredded Mozzarella cheese

¼ teaspoon dried oregano

¼ teaspoon garlic powder

½ teaspoon dried parsley

2 tablespoons grated vegetarian Parmesan cheese

Cut off 1 inch from the top and bottom of each courgette. Slice courgette in half lengthwise and use a spoon to scoop out a bit of the inside, making room for filling. Brush with oil and spoon 2 tablespoons pasta sauce into each shell. In a medium bowl, mix ricotta, Mozzarella, oregano, garlic powder, and parsley. Spoon the mixture into each courgette shell. Place stuffed courgette shells into the air fryer basket. Adjust the temperature to 176°C and air fry for 20 minutes. To remove from the basket, use tongs or a spatula and carefully lift out. Top with Parmesan. Serve immediately.

Lush Summer Rolls

Prep time: 15 minutes | Cook time: 15 minutes | Serves 4

235 ml shiitake mushroom, sliced thinly

1 celery stalk, chopped

1 medium carrot, shredded

½ teaspoon finely chopped ginger

1 teaspoon sugar

1 tablespoon soy sauce

1 teaspoon Engevita yeast flakes

8 spring roll sheets

1 teaspoon corn starch

2 tablespoons water

In a bowl, combine the ginger, soy sauce, Engevita yeast flakes, carrots, celery, mushroom, and sugar. Mix the cornflour and water to create an adhesive for the spring rolls. Scoop a tablespoonful of the vegetable mixture into the middle of the spring roll sheets. Brush the edges of the sheets with the cornflour adhesive and enclose around the filling to make spring rolls. Preheat the air fryer to 204°C. When warm, place the rolls inside and air fry for 15 minutes or until crisp. Serve hot.

Chapter 10 Desserts

Chapter 10 Desserts

Chocolate Chip Cookie Cake

Prep time: 5 minutes | Cook time: 15 minutes | Serves 8

4 tablespoons salted butter, melted	110 g blanched finely ground almond flour
65 g granular brown sweetener	½ teaspoon baking powder
1 large egg	40 g low-carb chocolate chips
½ teaspoon vanilla extract	

1. In a large bowl, whisk together butter, sweetener, egg, and vanilla. Add flour and baking powder and stir until combined. 2. Fold in chocolate chips, then spoon batter into an ungreased round nonstick baking dish. 3. Place dish into air fryer basket. Adjust the temperature to 148°C and set the timer for 15 minutes. When edges are browned, cookie cake will be done. 4. Slice and serve warm.

Pumpkin-Spice Bread Pudding

Prep time: 15 minutes | Cook time: 35 minutes | Serves 6

Bread Pudding:	1/3 loaf of day-old baguette or
175 ml heavy whipping cream	crusty country bread, cubed
120 g canned pumpkin	4 tablespoons unsalted butter,
80 ml whole milk	melted
65 g granulated sugar	Sauce:
1 large egg plus 1 yolk	80 ml pure maple syrup
½ teaspoon pumpkin pie spice	1 tablespoon unsalted butter
⅛ teaspoon kosher, or coarse	120 ml heavy whipping cream
sea salt	½ teaspoon pure vanilla extract

1. For the bread pudding: In a medium bowl, combine the cream, pumpkin, milk, sugar, egg and yolk, pumpkin pie spice, and salt. Whisk until well combined. 2. In a large bowl, toss the bread cubes with the melted butter. Add the pumpkin mixture and gently toss until the ingredients are well combined. 3. Transfer the mixture to a baking pan. Place the pan in the air fryer basket. Set the fryer to 176°C cooking for 35 minutes, or until custard is set in the middle. 4. Meanwhile, for the sauce: In a small saucepan, combine the syrup and butter. Heat over medium heat, stirring, until the butter melts. Stir in the cream and simmer, stirring often, until the sauce

has thickened, about 15 minutes. Stir in the vanilla. Remove the pudding from the air fryer. 5. Let the pudding stand for 10 minutes before serving with the warm sauce.

Crustless Peanut Butter Cheesecake

Prep time: 10 minutes | Cook time: 10 minutes | Serves 2

110 g cream cheese, softened	sugar-added peanut butter
2 tablespoons powdered	½ teaspoon vanilla extract
sweetener	1 large egg, whisked
1 tablespoon all-natural, no-	

1. In a medium bowl, mix cream cheese and sweetener until smooth. Add peanut butter and vanilla, mixing until smooth. Add egg and stir just until combined. 2. Spoon mixture into an ungreased springform pan and place into air fryer basket. Adjust the temperature to 148°C and bake for 10 minutes. Edges will be firm, but center will be mostly set with only a small amount of jiggle when done. 3. Let pan cool at room temperature 30 minutes, cover with plastic wrap, then place into refrigerator at least 2 hours. Serve chilled.

Baked Apple

Prep time: 10 minutes | Cook time: 20 minutes |
Makes 6 apple halves

3 small Pink Lady or other	3 tablespoons chopped pecans
baking apples	1 tablespoon firm butter, cut
3 tablespoons maple syrup	into 6 pieces

1. Put 6.5 tablespoons water in the drawer of the air fryer. 2. Wash apples well and dry them. 3. Split apples in half. Remove core and a little of the flesh to make a cavity for the pecans. 4. Place apple halves in air fryer basket, cut side up. 5. Spoon 1½ teaspoons pecans into each cavity. 6. Spoon ½ tablespoon maple syrup over pecans in each apple. 7. Top each apple with 1 piece of butter. 8. Bake at 184°C for 20 minutes, until apples are tender.

Blackberry Cobbler

Prep time: 15 minutes | Cook time: 25 to 30 minutes | Serves 6

330 g fresh or frozen blackberries	1 teaspoon vanilla extract
350 g granulated sugar, divided into 200 g and 150 g	8 tablespoons butter, melted
	125 g self-raising flour
	1 to 2 tablespoons oil

1. In a medium bowl, stir together the blackberries, 200 g of sugar, and vanilla. 2. In another medium bowl, stir together the melted butter, remaining 150 g of sugar, and flour until a dough forms. 3. Spritz a baking pan with oil. Add the blackberry mixture. Crumble the flour mixture over the fruit. Cover the pan with aluminum foil. 4. Preheat the air fryer to 176°C. 5. Place the covered pan in the air fryer basket. Cook for 20 to 25 minutes until the filling is thickened. 6. Uncover the pan and cook for 5 minutes more, depending on how juicy and browned you like your cobbler. Let sit for 5 minutes before serving.

Indian Toast and Milk

Prep time: 10 minutes | Cook time: 20 minutes | Serves 4

305 g sweetened, condensed milk	4 slices white bread
240 ml evaporated milk	2 to 3 tablespoons ghee or butter, softened
240 ml single cream	2 tablespoons crushed pistachios, for garnish (optional)
1 teaspoon ground cardamom, plus additional for garnish	
1 pinch saffron threads	

1. In a baking pan, combine the condensed milk, evaporated milk, half-and-half, cardamom, and saffron. Stir until well combined. 2. Place the pan in the air fryer basket. Set the air fryer to 176°C for 15 minutes, stirring halfway through the cooking time. Remove the sweetened milk from the air fryer and set aside. 3. Cut each slice of bread into two triangles. Brush each side with ghee. Place the bread in the air fryer basket. Keeping the air fryer on 176°C cook for 5 minutes or until golden brown and toasty. 4. Remove the bread from the air fryer. Arrange two triangles in each of four wide, shallow bowls. Pour the hot milk mixture on top of the bread and let soak for 30 minutes. 5. Garnish with pistachios if using, and sprinkle with additional cardamom.

Shortcut Spiced Apple Butter

Prep time: 5 minutes | Cook time: 1 hour | Makes 1¼ cups

Cooking spray	½ teaspoon kosher, or coarse sea salt
500 g store-bought unsweetened applesauce	¼ teaspoon ground cinnamon
130 g packed light brown sugar	⅛ teaspoon ground allspice
3 tablespoons fresh lemon juice	

1. Spray a cake pan with cooking spray. Whisk together all the ingredients in a bowl until smooth, then pour into the greased pan. Set the pan in the air fryer and bake at 172°C until the apple mixture is caramelized, reduced to a thick purée, and fragrant, about 1 hour. 2. Remove the pan from the air fryer, stir to combine the caramelized bits at the edge with the rest, then let cool completely to thicken. Scrape the apple butter into a jar and store in the refrigerator for up to 2 weeks.

Lush Chocolate Chip Cookies

Prep time: 7 minutes | Cook time: 9 minutes | Serves 4

3 tablespoons butter, at room temperature	chocolate
65 g light brown sugar, plus 1 tablespoon	¼ teaspoon baking soda
1 egg yolk	½ teaspoon vanilla extract
70 g plain flour	120 g semisweet chocolate chips
2 tablespoons ground white	Nonstick flour-infused baking spray

1. In medium bowl, beat together the butter and brown sugar until fluffy. Stir in the egg yolk. 2. Add the flour, white chocolate, baking soda, and vanilla and mix well. Stir in the chocolate chips. 3. Line a 6-by-2-inch round baking pan with baking paper. Spray the baking paper with flour-infused baking spray. 4. Insert the crisper plate into the basket and the basket into the unit. Preheat the unit to 148°C. 5. Spread the batter into the prepared pan, leaving a ½-inch border on all sides. 6. Once the unit is preheated, place the pan into the basket. 7. Bake to cookies for 9 minutes. 8. When the cooking is complete, the cookies should be light brown and just barely set. Remove the pan from the basket and let cool for 10 minutes. Remove the cookie from the pan, remove the baking paper, and let cool completely on a wire rack.

Brownies for Two

Prep time: 5 minutes | Cook time: 15 minutes | Serves 2

50 g blanched finely ground almond flour	½ teaspoon baking powder
3 tablespoons granulated sweetener	1 teaspoon vanilla extract
	2 large eggs, whisked
3 tablespoons unsweetened cocoa powder	2 tablespoons salted butter, melted

1. In a medium bowl, combine flour, sweetener, cocoa powder, and baking powder. 2. Add in vanilla, eggs, and butter, and stir until a thick batter forms. 3. Pour batter into two ramekins greased with cooking spray and place ramekins into air fryer basket. Adjust the temperature to 164°C and bake for 15 minutes. Centers will be firm when done. Let ramekins cool 5 minutes before serving.

Honeyed, Roasted Apples with Walnuts

Prep time: 5 minutes | Cook time: 12 to 15 minutes | Serves 4

2 Granny Smith apples	½ teaspoon ground cinnamon
20 g certified gluten-free rolled oats	2 tablespoons chopped walnuts
	Pinch salt
2 tablespoons honey	1 tablespoon olive oil

1. Preheat the air fryer to 192°C. 2. Core the apples and slice them in half. 3. In a medium bowl, mix together the oats, honey, cinnamon, walnuts, salt, and olive oil. 4. Scoop a quarter of the oat mixture onto the top of each half apple. 5. Place the apples in the air fryer basket, and roast for 12 to 15 minutes, or until the apples are fork tender.

Caramelized Fruit Skewers

Prep time: 10 minutes | Cook time: 3 to 5 minutes | Serves 4

2 peaches, peeled, pitted, and thickly sliced	½ teaspoon ground cinnamon
	¼ teaspoon ground allspice
3 plums, halved and pitted	Pinch cayenne pepper
3 nectarines, halved and pitted	Special Equipment:
1 tablespoon honey	8 metal skewers

1. Preheat the air fryer to 204°C. 2. Thread, alternating peaches, plums, and nectarines, onto the metal skewers that fit into the air fryer. 3. Thoroughly combine the honey, cinnamon, allspice, and cayenne in a small bowl. Brush the glaze generously over the fruit skewers. 4. Transfer the fruit skewers to the air fryer basket. You may need to cook in batches to avoid overcrowding. 5. Air fry for 3 to 5 minutes, or until the fruit is caramelized. 6. Remove from the basket and repeat with the remaining fruit skewers. 7. Let the fruit skewers rest for 5 minutes before serving.

Protein Powder Doughnut Holes

Prep time: 25 minutes | Cook time: 6 minutes | Makes 12 holes

50 g blanched finely ground almond flour	½ teaspoon baking powder
	1 large egg
60 g low-carb vanilla protein powder	5 tablespoons unsalted butter, melted
100 g granulated sweetener	½ teaspoon vanilla extract

1. Mix all ingredients in a large bowl. Place into the freezer for 20 minutes. 2. Wet your hands with water and roll the dough into twelve balls. 3. Cut a piece of baking paper to fit your air fryer basket. Working in batches as necessary, place doughnut holes into the air fryer basket on top of baking paper. 4. Adjust the temperature to 192°C and air fry for 6 minutes. 5. Flip doughnut holes halfway through the cooking time. 6. Let cool completely before serving.

Dark Chocolate Lava Cake

Prep time: 5 minutes | Cook time: 10 minutes | Serves 4

Olive oil cooking spray	½ teaspoon baking powder
30 g whole wheat flour	60 ml raw honey
1 tablespoon unsweetened dark chocolate cocoa powder	1 egg
	2 tablespoons olive oil
⅛ teaspoon salt	

1. Preheat the air fryer to 192°C. Lightly coat the insides of four ramekins with olive oil cooking spray. 2. In a medium bowl, combine the flour, cocoa powder, salt, baking powder, honey, egg, and olive oil. 3. Divide the batter evenly among the ramekins. 4. Place the filled ramekins inside the air fryer and bake for 10 minutes. 5. Remove the lava cakes from the air fryer and slide a knife around the outside edge of each cake. Turn each ramekin upside down on a saucer and serve.

Courgette Nut Muffins

Prep time: 15 minutes | Cook time: 15 minutes | Serves 4

60 ml vegetable oil, plus more for greasing	¼ teaspoon baking soda
90 g plain flour	¼ teaspoon baking powder
¾ teaspoon ground cinnamon	2 large eggs
¼ teaspoon kosher, or coarse sea salt	100 g granulated sugar
	90 g grated courgette
	35 g chopped walnuts

1. Generously grease four ramekins or a baking pan with vegetable oil. 2. In a medium bowl, sift together the flour, cinnamon, salt, baking soda, and baking powder. 3. In a separate medium bowl, beat together the eggs, sugar, and vegetable oil. Add the dry ingredients to the wet ingredients. Add the courgette and nuts and stir gently until well combined. Transfer the batter to the prepared ramekins or baking pan. 4. Place the ramekins or pan in the air fryer basket. Set the air fryer to 164ºC, and cook for 15 minutes, or until a cake tester or toothpick inserted into the center comes out clean. If it doesn't, cook for 3 to 5 minutes more and test again. 5. Let cool in the ramekins or pan on a wire rack for 10 minutes. Carefully remove from the ramekins or pan and let cool completely on the rack before serving.

Crispy Pineapple Rings

Prep time: 5 minutes | Cook time: 6 to 8 minutes | Serves 6

240 ml rice milk	½ teaspoon vanilla essence
85 g plain flour	½ teaspoon ground cinnamon
120 ml water	¼ teaspoon ground star anise
25 g unsweetened flaked coconut	Pinch of kosher, or coarse sea salt
4 tablespoons granulated sugar	1 medium pineapple, peeled and sliced
½ teaspoon baking soda	
½ teaspoon baking powder	

1. Preheat the air fryer to 192ºC. 2. In a large bowl, stir together all the ingredients except the pineapple. 3. Dip each pineapple slice into the batter until evenly coated. 4. Arrange the pineapple slices in the basket and air fry for 6 to 8 minutes until golden brown. 5. Remove from the basket to a plate and cool for 5 minutes before serving warm

Peanut Butter, Honey & Banana Toast

Prep time: 10 minutes | Cook time: 9 minutes | Serves 4

2 tablespoons unsalted butter, softened	2 bananas, peeled and thinly sliced
4 slices white bread	4 tablespoons honey
4 tablespoons peanut butter	1 teaspoon ground cinnamon

1. Spread butter on one side of each slice of bread, then peanut butter on the other side. Arrange the banana slices on top of the peanut butter sides of each slice (about 9 slices per toast). Drizzle honey on top of the banana and sprinkle with cinnamon. 2. Cut each slice in half lengthwise so that it will better fit into the air fryer basket. Arrange two pieces of bread, butter sides down, in the air fryer basket. Set the air fryer to 192ºC cooking for 5 minutes. Then set the air fryer to 204ºC and cook for an additional 4 minutes, or until the bananas have started to brown. Repeat with remaining slices. Serve hot.

Oatmeal Raisin Bars

Prep time: 15 minutes | Cook time: 15 minutes | Serves 8

40 g plain flour	50 g granulated sugar
¼ teaspoon kosher, or coarse sea salt	120 ml canola, or rapeseed oil
¼ teaspoon baking powder	1 large egg
¼ teaspoon ground cinnamon	1 teaspoon vanilla extract
50 g light brown sugar, lightly packed	110 g quick-cooking oats
	60 g raisins

1. Preheat the air fryer to 184ºC. 2. In a large bowl, combine the plain flour, kosher salt, baking powder, ground cinnamon, light brown sugar, granulated sugar, canola oil, egg, vanilla extract, quick-cooking oats, and raisins. 3. Spray a baking pan with nonstick cooking spray, then pour the oat mixture into the pan and press down to evenly distribute. Place the pan in the air fryer and bake for 15 minutes or until golden brown. 4. Remove from the air fryer and allow to cool in the pan on a wire rack for 20 minutes before slicing and serving.

Peaches and Apple Crumble

Prep time: 10 minutes | Cook time: 10 to 12 minutes | Serves 4

2 peaches, peeled, pitted, and chopped

1 apple, peeled and chopped

2 tablespoons honey

45 g quick-cooking oats

45 g whole-wheat pastry, or plain flour

2 tablespoons unsalted butter, at room temperature

3 tablespoons packed brown sugar

½ teaspoon ground cinnamon

1. Preheat the air fryer to 192°C. 2. Mix together the peaches, apple, and honey in a baking pan until well incorporated. 3. In a bowl, combine the oats, pastry flour, butter, brown sugar, and cinnamon and stir to mix well. Spread this mixture evenly over the fruit. 4. Place the baking pan in the air fryer basket and bake for 10 to 12 minutes, or until the fruit is bubbling around the edges and the topping is golden brown. 5. Remove from the basket and serve warm.

Printed in Great Britain
by Amazon

20943722R10041